Image OF A Black Father
Ode To the Sharecropper

Charlie Crane

We couldn't have done this without you. Words cannot express how thankful we are —
Love,
Matt & McKenzie

Copyright © 2007 by Charlie Crane

Image OF A Black Father
by Charlie Crane

Printed in the United States of America

ISBN 978-1-60266-657-3

All rights reserved solely by the author. The author guarantees all contents are original and do not infringe upon the legal rights of any other person or work. No part of this book may be reproduced in any form without the permission of the author. The views expressed in this book are not necessarily those of the publisher.

Unless otherwise indicated, Bible quotations are taken from New International Version .Copyright © 1990 by International Bible Society and Zondervan.

www.xulonpress.com

Acknowledgements

Jane Baker.. Writer

Sharon Frobra...................... Encouragement

Lisa Milligan .... Writer

Alberta Harrison................................. Writer

Lin Yeager-Sexton........................ Foreword

Jerry Cooper.......................... Cover Design

Rosetta Mines.......................... Final Details

Table of Contents

1. Sharecropping in Arkansas 9
2. Winter Comes to Arkansas 19
3. California or Bust 29
4. Reunited by the Bay 35
5. Grapes of Wrath 45
6. All Men Art Not Equal 55
7. Following Sherry 63
8. The Jesus Connection 75
9. Black Church / White Church 87
10. I Cain't Go to School! 93
11. Back to the Other Side of the Tracks 103
12. Coming Home 115
13. Memorial to the Sharecropper 125

Foreword

"Do not forsake me, O God, till I declare your power to the next generation"

Those are the Psalmist's words, but they could easily be Charlie Crane's, because in telling his own story Charlie has declared God's power in his own life: and I have a feeling God is pleased, even smiling, because He's rather partial to storytelling Himself.

Although this story is full of truth and drama: it's more than simply a record of a man who survived poverty, racism, and injustice. It's a story rich with living history, family loyalty and profound tragedy, yet vibrant with the joy of redemption.

To accompany Charlie on this journey is a true privilege, and it's an excursion that can only enrich our appreciation of what it means to be truly, fully, completely free.

Charlie's life is epigrammatic of an era. His boyhood world, though confined to a few square miles of farmland, held more wonder than the vastness of today's childhood vistas.

The immense respect and admiration he had for his elders, and his father Jab in particular, formed Charlie's character.

And who knows, because of Charlie's circle of influence how many folks, have embraced Jab Crane's wisdom through the years, never even knowing Jab himself?

Certainly, Charlie Crane's sharecropper dad could never have imagined how his life would affect more folks than those in his own sizable family. He could never have realized how his legacy of integrity, strength, and humility would be magnified in Charlie's life and passed on to hundreds if not thousands of people through Charlie's life as a husband, father, foster father, employee, mentor and pastor.

Jab's father-in-law, Paw, was the teller of stories, the keeper of the family narrative. As Charlie's youth was spent in a world without broadcast media, his family story was crafted, polished, told and retold, savored and appreciated. Did Jab Crane know his boy Charlie studied his every move, idolizing him for his quiet strength and faithfulness to his family? Did he understand how the repeated telling of the family story gave young Charlie a sense of worth in a coldly segregated world? And did Jab grasp the fact that Charlie's life would bridge two disparate worlds and become a bridge for blacks and whites to traverse together?

Today Charlie's personal story is the continuation of the Crane legacy, reminding us that our own family stories are important and must be told.

When I sat down to read this book, Kleenex ready, tearfully amazed, I discovered my own name. Memory jogged, I remembered casting Charlie in *FREEMAN*, my first produced play. It's just like God, in His kindness, to encourage us with reminders that our lives do indeed touch others in meaningful ways. What's more, for Charlie to have been blessed – even changed – as he played the chained slave in *FREEMAN* its both humbling and astonishing to me. Our lives do intersect, but sometimes we have to have Gods perspective to see the junction.

Image OF A Black Father

I don't know if my father realized the impact of his own unquestioning, natural acceptance of Charlie. I know Dad respected and admired him, was his mentor and cheerleader. In reading this book, its clear that Dads love for Charlie reached beyond the finiteness of both their lives. When Dad met Charlie that day at First Baptist Modesto, he saw the soul of a man who'd come through the fire, a man with great potential, and one whose scars God cherished. Dad knew Charlie's life was a sermon in itself and he was glad to help get the word out.

In his introduction to the book of Exodus, Eugene Peterson says, "God does not present us with salvation in the form of abstract truth, or a precise definition or a catchy slogan, but a story." This book is part of that ongoing story of salvation. I don't know how your life will be touched by it, but I do know you hold a treasure in your hand.

Lin Yaeger Sexton
Modesto, California

Chapter One

Sharecropping in Arkansas

Even as a three-year-old boy, I could appreciate my dad, sharecropping a farm amidst the beauty of tall cypress trees growing along the riverbanks outside Dumas, Arkansas. On a typical morning in March or early April, the season of plowing and planting for sharecroppers, this giant of a man I called Dad, his shoulders muscle bound from working the land, slipped out of bed while the roosters still crowed. He slid his legs into his overhauls, hauling the straps up over his shoulders, laced up his old boots, went out and harnessed the mule to get ready to plow. He left the house without breakfast, because he didn't want to wake my mother to cook for him. He let her sleep.

I'd slip out of my bed and tag along with Dad most days, watching him work for a couple of hours.

Dad, whose nickname was Jab, took his customary matches from the matchbox over the stove and put them into his shirt pocket to light his cigarettes, rolled from a can of Prince Albert tobacco. We went out to the barn and hitched the mule together, and he smoked as we walked out to the field.

We'd go on past the gnarly roots of the cypress trees running over the bank and down into the water of the river. Trees formed the boundary lines that separated one plantation from another. There were large wooded areas where tall hickory, oak, pine and cedar trees grew, forming a roof over rich, untilled soil. Much of the dirt was untouched, yet grew wild grapes, berries and other fruits and nuts to feed the animals that lived in Arkansas. The sweet smell of wildflowers, honeysuckle, buttercups and blooming trees would start bees humming and birds singing the joyful sounds of spring. That smell could even send a boy singing.

Dad and the mule would cut through the dirt of the field, back and forth, back and forth.

Later in the morning, the muggy air grew hot, and Dad started to sweat. His matches got wet. He couldn't strike them, so he reached in his back pocket and pulled out a cut of Days Work chewing tobacco. However, tobacco wasn't his only interest while he worked.

Motioning for me to come to him, he said, "Charlie, take the bucket down to the river and get us something cool to drink."

I thought, *My Daddy can drink a lot of water.* I loved to take water to my father. Some days I hauled two buckets. I was little, but I lugged two five-pound buckets.

I grabbed two now and ran to the river. Once they were full, I struggled with them over the plowed ground to take the water, one for Jab and one for the mule. They could both drink about the same amount. Then I sat down to study my dad while he plowed.

I'd think to himself, *when I grow up I'm going to smoke Prince Albert tobacco, and I'm going to chew my Days Work. I'm going to plow my mule, and I'm going to be just like Daddy.*

Our mother, Cordie, had three boys before me. My oldest brother was named Albert. His name hadn't anything to do

Image OF A Black Father

with the Prince Albert tobacco, but he was named Albert. Jab and Cordie named their second boy John after my mother's uncle. Our grandfather, Bud, also had a brother named John. Cordie and St. Clair named their third son St. Clair, Jr. Cordie badly wanted her fourth child to be a girl. She made up her mind whether a girl or a boy came, this child would work in the house helping with inside chores, the washing, ironing, that sort of work. The fourth child was me. They named me after Jab's uncle, Charles Currie. Charles Currie was the one who had lovingly named St. Clair, my dad, Jab.

Two years later, my sister, Dorothy, was born. Cordie, when Dorothy (Dot) grew old enough, started to train both her and me to do the chores around the house.

Dot wasn't much help at doing the chores, but she provided a lot of company. Her mouth moved constantly, and I could appreciate that. We grew up together, with the same responsibilities.

The first was learning how to feed the small animals we raised on the farm for food. We fed the chickens, slopped the pigs and made sure the cow had water. Our chores also included milking the cow twice a day, getting eggs from the hen house every evening and churning butter once a week.

One day we started off to milk the cow, Dot dancing along, her plaits bouncing. I thought, *I always have to take this dumb bucket. I wish she'd take a turn now and then.* Being the only girl among all her brothers, Dot was something of a tomboy. She wore the same cut-offs and cotton shirts the boys wore. Now and then in the golden sun of the new morning, she'd run barefooted as far up the trunk of a tree as gravity would allow and then jump back to the ground. "Charlie," she asked, her words jumbling together with the speed of her talk, "How come de buddah be yella —when de milk be white?"

"I don' know. You proly need to ast the cow," I replied.

How was I supposed to answer a cockamamie question like that.

When we got to the barn, the cats lined up by the brown cow hoping I would shoot them some milk. Dot scooped a little grain in the manger, and I set the three-legged stool next to the cow's udder. The milk hitting the metal bucket at first sounded like quiet thunder, and then turned to a swish, swish as the bucket filled up. Dot circled around to the other side of the cow and started pulling teats. She never did this very long because she only got dribbles, but at least this way she could say she helped. When the cow's udder was empty we let her back into the meadow, and I lugged the bucket to the house.

Together Dot and I lifted the bucket of milk up to the top of the cabinet and covered it with a clean flour sack towel. While we waited for the cream to come to the top, we went out to the porch and hauled in some more wood for the fire.

"If you wasn't a sharecropper's boy what would you be?" Dot asked as we lugged in the cut logs. I didn't answer.

I knew she really wanted to tell me what she'd be if she weren't a sharecropper's daughter. Sure enough, "I know what I'd be," she said. "I'd be one of them store ladies in Dumas. I'd sell clothes and shoes, and I'd have so many pretty things to wear people would turn around and look at me go by."

"Proly get them things pretty torn up if you climbed trees in them," I observed.

Dot whacked me with a stick of kindling. "Well ya' durn fool," she said, "I wouldn' climb no trees if I had that kind of finery."

After a few hours we pulled the flour sack from the milk and skimmed the cream off, turning a serving spoon sideways so we didn't get much milk with the cream. Dot took the lid off the little churn, and I dumped the cream in, then put the lid back on and started pumping up and down. Dot settled in Cordie's rocker and rocked as far back and forth as it would go.

"Do you want to stay in Arkansas forever, Charlie?" she asked. "I'd like to leave here, go off and see what else is in the world. I'd like to see St. Louis."

"At's not likely," I answered, still pumping up and down.

"How do you know? You ain't the king," she answered, her eyes afar off imagining the big city in her mind.

Again I didn't respond.

"My turn," Dot said, and churned for about two minutes. Rubbing her shoulders, she whined, "My arms are tired, you take a turn." She had already stopped churning and I went to pushing up and down. After an eternity, little yellow flecks of butter sloshed around in the cream. Luckily for me, about that time our mother came in from the fields. She took the ball of butter out and kneaded it to remove all the milk.

While Dot and I were young, our Great Grandmother Josephine came to live with us. She was old, and had rheumatism, so part of our chores were to care for her.

One day she wanted to wash clothes. "Dot, Charlie, I'll pay ya'll to tote me some watah from the river so I can wash," she called.

We thought we'd get candy or maybe a few coins, so we went back and forth hauling water until the pot was full. When we were done, Grandma Josephine pulled a plug of Brown Mule chewing tobacco out and pinched off a piece for each of us.

"Daddy gonna' whup us if we chew this bacca," I whispered.

"Let's jus' taste it," Dot responded. "We're not gonna' tell."

We both spent the rest of the day sick as a dog.

However, Grandma Josephine lived in a room that opened to the back of the house about five feet up from the river. We decided to take revenge on the old lady. We hauled some more water from the river and poured it at her door with the intention of pushing her down the hill into the river. Unknown to us, Josephine stood at her window watching us turn her doorway into mud. She didn't come out at all, even though we waited and waited. When the grownups came home from the field, we ran for padding for our pants.

Our grandfather, Paw, saved us, though. Just as Jab said, "Bend Over, Charlie," and I responded, "Yes suh," Paw said, "Served her right. She shouldn't have given those kids chewing tobacco." That was the end of the spanking. Dot ran outside before she allowed herself to clap her hands and laugh.

As Dot and I grew a little older, we were given more responsibilities, such as washing clothes. Every Monday doing the laundry took up a whole day. We hauled water up from the river, bucket-by-bucket, my two to Dot's half. We filled a large black iron wash pot set on three bricks. We heated the water by setting fire to wood we'd piled around the bottom of the pot.

Dot whined, "I'm hot, and my arms is sore," while we soaked the clothes in hot boiling water, the white clothes especially.

"The quicker you get on wid it, the quicker you'll be done," I answered.

Once the pot was filled with clothes, we put in lye soap and bleached or boiled the clothes white.

Next we took them out of the wash pot and put them into a tub of warm water where we used a rub board on them. We rubbed and rubbed on this board to the tune of Dot's complaining, until we got all the clothes clean. Then we rinsed them. If the clothes were white, we put bluing in them to make them even whiter. Finally, we hung them out on the line.

Image OF A Black Father

About the time Dot was five and I was seven, a new brother joined the Crane family. His name was Eston Delano. His middle name came from Franklin Delano Roosevelt, the president of the whole United States. Jab and Cordie had their way of getting names for their children. Eston presented another problem for Dot and me because we had to learn how to baby-sit. We had to learn how to keep this little guy clean, including changing his diapers. There were no Pampers in those days. We had to change cloth diapers. We had to wash diapers. We even hid diapers so we wouldn't have to wash them. We had to keep this little guy clean all the time, and he remained a real problem.

Not only did we have to look after Eston, our family had a wood-burning stove that our mom taught Dot and me to cook on. We had to keep wood in the stove to keep the fire going while we boiled beans or whatever the evening meal was going to be. We distracted each other some days, either letting the fire go out, or burning the beans by getting it too hot, or not stirring enough. Play was not rewarded in the Crane family, responsibility was. Dot and I paid the price for ruining a meal with "blistered" bottoms.

One fall day Cordie went to help gather crops with the rest of the family. She came home to get the noon meal started, but first, she rubbed coal oil on her bleeding hands to clean them, and then she put Vaseline on to heal the cuts picking the cotton had made. "Charlie, you and Dot are doing a good job today," she said. "You keep at it. I expect we'll be back in about two hours. Have the table set and the milk poured when the sun's straight up. We wont' have much time to eat. We've got to get this cotton picked. There's rain clouds coming." With that, she left for the field again.

We proudly finished cooking dinner while she went back to the field. That was a no spanking day.

The noon meal was called dinner, the evening meal supper. At breakfast our family ate a heavy meal, like biscuits, gravy and rice or another heavy food, pork chops, squirrel, or whatever. The family would have a heavy dinner at noon, sweet potatoes or boiled beans and cornbread. At suppertime we ate light. Sometimes we drank a glass of buttermilk and ate a piece of cornbread, just one baked sweet potato, or maybe our grandmother would bake a pie. She loved to bake pies, and we would have pie and a glass of milk.

On another day, dinner went all right, but while making supper, Dot and I got to playing.

"How come women have so many children?" she said, her hands on her hips. "They eat too much, and dirty up too many dishes and clothes. If there was only a few youngens', then washin' and cleanin' would be easier." "Who should leave?" I asked.

"You, to start with!"

"You couldn't live without me, and you know it."

We collapsed in laughter, and spent the whole afternoon thinking on who would have to go. About the time we came to the conclusion that people would have to limit children *before* they were born, because after they were here you loved them too much, we heard Dad's voice from the road. We hadn't gotten our chores done, and the light had faded to evening. Our family were heading home expecting to eat and expecting the cow not to be mooing her head off because her udder was bursting. We quietly slunk off to pad our pants again because we knew we were going to get a spanking.

There were no child abuse laws in those days, and the older folks didn't mind spanking a youngen to get him or her back on track. One thing's sure, that infraction didn't happen again the next day. There was a lot of love in those spankings, though. The old folks spanked the children, but they loved them and trained them in the right way.

Dot and I were taught to have respect for authority, for our parents, and older siblings. We stood at the bottom of the pecking order, except for Eston, so we had to respect everyone in the family. Anyone we didn't respect could give us a spanking as well. Of course, though I was older than Dot, she didn't respect anything I said. I had no authority over her.

The chores we shared together bonded us. We learned how to fight and argue with one another, without hurting each other. When we got into trouble, we laughed at each other. I would laugh when Dot got a spanking. Dot would laugh when I got a spanking. When times were good we'd laugh together. We had fun. Dot was my best friend. Our chores made us know we were needed in the family. The Crane family lived a hardworking good life. Even so, we children had a lot to learn.

Chapter Two

Winter Comes to Arkansas

When cotton picking time passed, and the days turned colder, the rhythms of life changed for my family. After a typical work day, the cows came home, drank water, and settled down for the night; the mule was put away in the stall, rubbed down, fed and watered; the chickens gathered in the henhouse to roost, the pigs all quieted down. When we sharecroppers had readied the farm for night and begun to hear the whippoorwills sing, the crickets rub their legs together, the lightning bugs flitter in the air, after we'd eaten supper and washed and put away the dishes, family time would start just at the dusk of dark.

If the weather was fitting, my family usually gathered around what we called a "smoke." We put leaves and grass on a fire to make it smoke because the smoke warded off mosquitoes. Usually the smoke burned where the old wash pot normally sat.

The old people would start talking there in the dark. They told the stories, the history of our culture. This family time served as our only entertainment. No one had radios or TVs. Instead, we listened to the older people. Sometimes we'd sing, sometimes talk, whatever the mood dictated, that's what we did. It was a time when the family really turned together and felt each other's needs and concerns.

On the other hand, if the weather were bad, or the mosquitoes unwilling to cooperate, we gathered inside. We had the wood-burning potbelly stove in the corner that we lit and congregated around when it was cool.

This part of the day always focused on Mom's father. She called him Papa. All the grandchildren called him Paw. His friends called him Bud, but his name was Arthur Jackson. The oldest male in the family always told the stories. Paw was the oldest, and he was the storyteller. He was six foot three, bald, and wore overalls, like Jab, but Paw wore his BVDs under his overalls.

Paw would trim a stick to make a toothpick, and he would have the toothpick ready for storytelling.

For the last story before we went to bed, Paw usually told the family one of his wild mystery jokes to give us something to pray about. He believed in afterlife, haints, voodoo. He believed in a lot of things, but he called himself a Christian. One of the stories he used to tell was about how Whiskey Slough got its name.

I remember the first night I heard the story of Whiskey Slough. Paw reared back in his chair so that only two legs were still on the floor, and in a low voice began, "There was a beautiful woman of the night who worked in bars and ran a rooming house in town. She lived in the country and had to cross the little slough in a ravine on her way to work or to town. She would cross the bridge, work the weekend, then come home half drunk. She loved whiskey. One weekend night, she was returning home when her horse spooked at something, ran off the side of the bridge, her buggy turned over in the slough and she drowned."

Paw stopped for effect, looking slowly around the family, catching the eyes of each child, and then continued, "Thereafter, every time someone carrying whiskey tried to cross the bridge where she was killed, they couldn't pass. Something would stop them, blow a warm breath in their face, and leave them helpless to move across that bridge. If they drove a horse and buggy, the horse would come unharnessed from the buggy, walk out on the bridge, and they would have to reconnect the horse to the wagon. When they tried to move again, they would stop, and the horse would walk out again. If they rode on horseback, the horse would stop and refuse to cross the bridge." Paw took out his toothpick, sucked on his tooth, hung the toothpick in the other side of his mouth, and said, "Since I cross this bridge when I come from town, I keep a little somethin', usually a bottle of whiskey, ready. When I get to the bridge over the slough, I stop, get off Red, pour a drink of whiskey in a cup and set it down. I can hear the woman lapping the whiskey from the cup."

At the end of the story Paw came back down on the four legs of his chair with a thump, and that was the children's signal to get to bed.

Paw always told our family, "There is a spiritual world out there. You've got to be aware of it. There are evil spirits and there are good spirits. You've got to know that there is a spiritual world." We children would go to bed and pray that the evil spirits wouldn't bother us.

Jab's conversations during the smoke were of a more serious nature. He'd tap a stick on the floor and tell us the history of his own life. One time he said, "I didn't have no sisters and brothers. After Daddy died, it was just me and Mama."

Dot crawled up on his lap, and asked, "Where was you borned?"

"Right here in Dumas."

The curious Dot asked another question, "Well, *when* was you born, Daddy?"

"September 8, 1897. I only went to the third grade because I had to work with my Mama. She'd put on ol' high-top shoes and we'd hitch up the ol' mule. We'd plow all day, from sun up to sundown. I always wanted to go to school, but I never did."

Jab laughed, "I did learn how to ride a wheel, though. When we was in town one day, Mom was in the store, and I was settin' outside watchin' a white boy ride a wheel. After he passed by a couple of times, he asked me would I like to ride his wheel. Dad blame! I said I surely would. In little or no time, this little boy showed me how to ride the wheel. I never owned a wheel of my own, but I always wanted to. One day ya'll are gonna' own, and learn to ride, a wheel."

Dot snuggled in Dad's elbow, "What's a wheel, Daddy?" she asked.

"Why, it's called a bicycle, now, Girl. Ain't you seen one in Dumas?"

"Oh, sure, I seen that," Dot lied, bobbing her head up and down. I could always tell when she was puttin' on.

Riding a bicycle was only one of the things he imagined he wanted his children to do. He'd point at us with his stick and say, "I want you children to go to school, and I want at least one of you boys to finish school, so you can do business on the same level as the white man."

Many nights Jab repeated, "Guns and knives are used for hunting and gathering food for the table, not for protection. I never carry a gun or a knife for protection, because some fool will make me use them. I'd wind up killin' somebody, or they'd kill me. Either way, I lose. I don't carry protection. The only protection I used growing up, and even now, is a soft answer. Whenever you are asked a question, especially by a white man, answer softly." He would lean back on the rear legs of his chair, like Paw did, and add, "You boys do not look at, talk to, or touch a white girl. These things are bad and could cost you your life. They will hang you."

Then there were the nights he explained to his children, "How I love workin'. I like bein' by myself, workin' hard, talkin' to the mule and God. Hard work never hurt anybody. It keeps this ol' body in shape. It keeps you strong and sturdy. My back kind of aches sometimes, but that's OK." He'd hook his thumbs in his suspenders and continue, "Sharecroppin' is not a bad thing. Right now, it's the only thing, but if you can ever find something else to do that's better, then do it. Whatever you do, do it the best you can." Then he would tell us about some of the jobs he used to have.

He'd throw back his head and remember, "I once had a job that took me across the Mason-Dixon Line." The Mason-Dixon Line is a line drawn by Mr. Mason and Mr. Dixon that separates the northern and southern states. "I loaded and unloaded boxcars on a freight train that took me from Dumas to St. Louis, Missouri. Sometimes I stayed in St. Louis. Sometimes I came back to Dumas the same day. St. Louis, now, there is a city. Man, I love that city.

Colored people can go wherever they want to go, even into the movie theatre without being told to leave.

"Not like here in Dumas, where you have to set upstairs and watch the picture show. Here, you know, you've seen, they don't clean where the colored people set. Nobody ever goes up there, so it's trashy and dirty. But you go on up there, and you watch the picture show. When you leave, you leave the same way; go down the outside steps and home. But in St. Louis — in St. Louis you can walk right through the front door. You are able to buy popcorn, candy, peanuts, the whole bit. You can set wherever you want to, and the theatre is clean. The ushers take you to a seat. The seats are soft and plush.

"In Dumas, there ain't no place to try on clothes. They don't have dressin' rooms for colored people. You just have to know your size. In St. Louis, you can take the clothes right in the dressin' room and try them on, buy them to fit. In Dumas you can't try on shoes. I went into a shoe store, and started to try on a pair of shoes.

The clerk told me, 'You put your black foot in that shoe; I won't be able to sell it. If you try it on, by god, you better buy it.' In St. Louis you can go into a store and try on a pair of shoes. Buy them if you want to. If they don't fit, you don't have to buy them."

My brothers and sisters and I wanted to do all of these *free* things; go anywhere we wanted, sit anywhere we wanted. We longed to cross the Mason-Dixon Line. Jab talked quite often about going North.

In late summer living was easy. The crops were growing, and the sharecroppers had to cultivate them once in a while, but the difficult, painful work of fall cotton chopping had passed, and wouldn't be back, for a while, at least. The cotton was growing high, now. The gardens produced fruit. Cordie, Ma, Dot and I were in the middle of the canning season. We canned the vegetables for winter. We canned peaches, too. Dot and I learned how to wash jars, peel peaches, cook the fruit for canning and seal the jars so they wouldn't let any air in to spoil the fruit.

There I was, doing all this inside work, while my brothers went fishing, hunting or enjoyed other pursuits. I would much have preferred their ways of contributing to the family.

Dot and I got a lot of play times in the afternoons, though. We played out where the dust lay deep in the roads and up the roadsides. Instead of making sand castles, we made dust castles. We made all kinds of designs in the dust, houses, cars or whatever. One day we made a dust model of a car and left it in the middle of the road. Not many folks came down our road, so it wasn't in anyone's way.

This car production happened on a Friday. Paw had gone to town that evening, and he came walking back that night having had a couple of drinks.

Grandma Lucinda told us later that she heard him say, "Dag nab it. What is that in the road?" she got out of bed to see what was going on and saw him stagger a few steps closer to the model of the car Dot and I had made in the dust.

"That's a durn bobcat," he said, "crouched down waitin' to leap on me." In the dim moonlight, he eased his knife out of his pocket, opened it and decided, "I'm going to jump this cat before it jumps me." He heaved himself into the pile of dust yelling, fighting, kicking and hollering. "Ha! Think you're going to take Arthur Jackson, you got another think comin', cat!"

He made such a commotion our grandmother was worried he'd wake us all up. "Oh, my Lord, what's gotten into that man now," she said quietly, hoping not to wake the rest of the family, who were already wide awake. Dot and I saw her climb out of bed and the tail of her nightgown catch in the door as she rushed out to pull Paw out of the dusty road. The door opened again slightly as she pulled her nightgown off a splinter.

After a bit, she came back in with him leaning on her as if she was big and he was little. All the time she washed him up and put him to bed, he whispered loudly that if she'd just let him loose, he'd go back and give that bobcat what for and how come.

"You jus' come on and get a little rest first," Grandma said as she tucked him in.

Paw and the "bobcat" were the joke of the year for us. We took turns telling the story and laughing about Paw and the bobcat for years.

Needless to say, our family was poor. Poverty didn't complicate life for us, though. Life was simple. We could find a way to laugh at just about anything. We were so poor, the house we lived in had a tin roof. It leaked like a sieve with the slightest rain, but we laughed at the house. Paw would say, "This house has so many cracks in the wall, we could put the cat out without opening the door! We can just throw him through a crack." Everyone in the family copied Paw's one or two liners.

Having no money also affected clothes. Everything we wore was made of the cotton we grew, as well as our quilts and mattresses.

Mom would add to our fabric by buying flour in a 50 pound sack, and then take those sacks and make dresses for the girls, shirts for the boys, even underwear.

We also had this little outhouse that sat way out from the main house because our house had no plumbing. In the wintertime we wore BVDs. BVDs were a brand of long johns that had a little flap in the back that was held up by three buttons, so that when we went to the outhouse we didn't have to strip off all our clothes, just unbutton this flap in the back. These BVDs were a very convenient thing because there was no heater in the outhouse, and it was cold.

On a typical night, Dot said, "Charlie unbutton me," and she raced for the outhouse, making it just in time. When she came back, I said, "OK, your turn." She unbuttoned me, and I raced for the little house. A great convenience, those BVDs.

In winter, my brothers and sisters and I also wore cotton stockings, not socks. The stockings came all the way up to our knees, and we wore rubber boots with them.

We would go to school this way, dressed up in many warm clothes. We had to, because it got below freezing in Arkansas.

Our school and church were the same whitewashed, one-room building. All twelve grades, pre-primer (kindergarten) through twelfth grade learned in one room. Mrs. Taylor, teacher for pre-primer through sixth grade, taught her students at one end. A big potbelly stove in the middle of the room stood like an iron sentry separating the elementary children from junior high and high school students. On the upper grade end of the room, Mr. Johnson taught all the kids in seventh through twelfth grade. Albert and John were the only two Crane children taught by Mr. Johnson. Everything came secondhand, the books, the desks, the pencils, some even thought the teachers. We had no electricity at school, so we burned kerosene lamps, like we did at home.

Dot and I didn't see many white kids, except when the white children came and went from school on big yellow buses that passed the Crane children, who walked to school.

Sometimes the youngest of us Cranes would ride the mule if the weather were too bad for the mule to work. One day on the way to school I stepped on the mule's foot. Well, that mule stepped right back. He wouldn't get off my foot even though I hollered, "Dad blame it, get off my foot!" and threw myself every which direction trying to get loose. My foot hurt like crazy, but I had to stay at school all that day. When we finally rode the mule home, my foot was swollen about as big as Dad's. Mom soaked it in ice.

The good thing about the wintertime was that the family had even less chores to do than in late summer. The older people took over the children's chores of feeding the little animals and doing the washing. I liked when it snowed so much we couldn't walk to school. The other thing I liked about winter was Christmas. Christmas was the best time of the year. Oh, Christmas was something. We had goose for Christmas, not turkey.

About two or three weeks before Christmas we penned the goose up, feeding it nothing but grain, so it would be cleaned out and solid meat. We cooked up cakes and pies for Christmas, too.

Christmas morning came and we children opened our Christmas shoeboxes. We'd find an apple or orange, some hard peppermint candies, nuts, pecans, walnuts and hickory nuts, put there by our parents. They packed those boxes with love. We hardly ever got a toy, but when we did we cherished it. Every once in a while I would get a cap gun. There were a thousand things to shoot with a cap gun. Usually we got new sweaters, and had a chance to show off our new clothes at the church Christmas program. We stood up in front of everyone and said a poem or something else we'd memorized. For instance:

When I was little boy just so high
My mama would take a switch and make me cry
Now I'm a big boy and Mama can't do it
But Papa take a big switch and get right to it

Poems, things we'd made up, things that caused people to laugh. We had a great time.

Later at home, people came by to share their Christmas stories or gifts, or eat goose and dressing, or cake that our grandmother and mother had cooked for Christmas. Paw liked Christmas because it gave him another excuse for having his Christmas cheer around. He had his eggnog in little bottles stashed here and there so he could take a little drink now and then. He wasn't an alcoholic. He just liked to drink on certain occasions. Grandmother Lucinda was a great Christian, and she read the family Christmas stories. Christmas in the Crane household was a joyful time. But a time was coming, that would change the Crane family's life forever.

Chapter Three

California or Bust

Dad was a middle-aged man by the time the Japanese drew the United States into World War II in 1941 with the bombing of Pearl Harbor. However, being the middle-aged father of a large family didn't stop him from hoping his vision of moving to a northern state, a free state, to make a better life for his wife and children might become a reality. His age kept him out of the service, but he wasn't too old to help in the war effort. Going north would provide him that opportunity, however his vision needed help and planning. Maybe the adults planned when Dot, my other brothers and I had gone to bed, but not before. The folks never discussed it in front of the children, especially not around the smoke. If one of us had slipped, and a landowner had learned of Jab's intention to move to California, they'd have forced Jab into indebtedness that kept us all in Arkansas, forever.

Cousin Minner, a nephew of Paw's, and Cordie's first cousin, was called Minner because he was of small stature, five foot five or six, small like the minnow is to the fish family. His name was actually Lee Arthur Lewis. A young rake without many obligations, he left his farm without anyone noticing or saying anything, because he wasn't sharecropping on his own. Minner, who dressed snappy, wore a pencil-thin mustache, a gold tooth and enjoyed lots of girl friends, made it all the way to California. In 1943, soon after he got to the coast, he and Jab started making plans for us to move out there, too. Cousin Minner directed and financed Jab's first trip, and also helped him find a job in California, all unknown to us Crane children.

Because of the necessary secrecy, the day that Jab left home for California caught me completely by surprise. I hadn't known anything was going on. Now, Jab was packing clothes in his old suitcase, hugging us all and kissing Cordie goodbye.

"Why you goin' to leave us?" I asked, already feeling a puddle of tears in my eyes.

"I'm going to California to find a better life for us," Dad answered. "I'll come back to get ya'll as soon as I'm set up."

I had watched Jab closely, loved him, made him my hero, but now Jab was leaving. I didn't understand any of this. I only knew Jab was leaving. It was the worst day of my life.

"Daddy," I cried, when Jab threw his suitcase into the back of the car. "Daddy, don't go." I lit out to run into the dusty road, but my mother's voice stopped me.

"No, Charlie," she said. "Dad has to go alone. He'll come back for us."

Jab leaned out the window and called, "You take care of your mama, now."

Surging forward, I screamed, "Come back, Daddy." My brother grabbed me around my chest and picked me up off the ground. I kicked and struggled, but my brother held tight.

I felt furious at not being able to get loose. At the same time I felt desperate. In my whole life I'd never been separated from Jab over one day at a time. I thought Jab would be gone forever.

Image OF A Black Father

Paw stood with us in the road, watching Jab slowly disappear and me struggle and yell for my father. Paw told good stories and helped took care of the family and oversaw things, but he would never be able to replace Jab. I glanced at my grandfather, then back at my father's disappearing car. Jab was the hero, especially my hero, and my hero was about to disappear down the road. The car became a little dot and then became invisible over a knoll. My brother let me down. I kicked at the dust and thought, *How could a father leave his son for any reason, even to go to California.* The day that Jab left was a hole in my world.

It took about seven days and a three-cent stamp for a letter to travel from California to Arkansas. Someone from the family checked the post office in Dumas once a week, since it was a five-mile walk to town.

After several weeks of anxiously waiting, Cordie received a letter general delivery from Jab. She gathered us all around her and read Jab's letter aloud. This letter, and all the letters that followed, began with the same salutation: "Dear Honey, Just a few lines to let you hear from me. This letter leaves me fine, and I hope it finds you the same." After a brief description of his journey to the West, and a statement about finding a job in Oakland, California, he closed the letter by saying, "Tell everyone hello for me, and give my love to the children. I will close this letter until I hear from you again. Yours truly, S.C. Crane, p.s. I miss all of you." This was good. Jab had never had to write letters before, so he had never tried to express his feelings on paper. He had never tried to paint a picture about what things were really like for him, or explain the difference between the lifestyle in California versus that of Arkansas. He was experiencing both a new world and how to describe it to his family.

His later letters told how Jab learned many new things. He learned to drive a car and got a driver's license.

He explored the streets, and found his way around the city. He learned to like Lucky Strike cigarettes instead of Prince Albert tobacco. He still had his Day's Work, though. He'd chew his Day's Work when he was at home.

One letter said Jab had landed a job in the Navy shipyard in Alameda, California, where he had to learn how to work with different people up close. He dressed differently and took orders from a supervisor, too. Everything was different for him, and he had to learn all these things in a short amount of time.

After about a year, Jab was settled in his new life. He felt comfortable with his job and had his own place now. He took vacation time to come back to Arkansas, visit with us, and make plans for our future when the rest of us moved to California. He brought pictures and postcards of the Bay Area where he had settled, as well as a kaleidoscope and viewer. He told us about the Bay Bridge, one of the longest in the world, and the Alameda tunnel that went under the bay.

Another child, Willie, was born into their family that first year, 1944, while Jab was away in California. Now that Jab was back in Arkansas, he saw his newborn son for the first time, the last of his children to be born in Arkansas. He also took Dot and me down to Shreveport, Louisiana on a vacation to see Pauline, his firstborn daughter, who was married now. She and her husband were preparing to migrate from Arkansas to Toledo, Ohio, which they did that same year. This was a farewell trip for all of them.

Dot and I took our first bus ride. We had to sit in the back of the bus behind the yellow line where all the colored people sat. We also had to stay overnight in New Dora, Arkansas, because the buses only ran in the daytime. The bus driver stopped the bus before sundown, everybody got off, and he said, "We'll be spending the night here. You've got to be here tomorrow morning by 8:00." Then he told Jab,

Image OF A Black Father

"The colored quarters are that way," and he pointed across the railroad tracks.

We had to walk several blocks, maybe close to a mile, to get to the colored part of town. When we arrived, there was a sign that said, "Rooming House" in front of a colored lady's home. We paid $.50 to spend the night with that family and get breakfast the next morning. Sleeping in someone else's bed excited Dot and me, because we'd never been away from home or stayed with anyone before. We hurried back down to the bus station the next morning before 8 a.m. and continued our trip to Shreveport.

Though I had met my sister, Pauline, before, she'd been a teenager. I was her favorite brother then. Now, I thought Pauline was the tallest, skinniest woman I'd ever seen. She was as tall as Jab.

"Oh," she said, "Charlie, my baby," and she hugged me.

We visited sunup to sundown, catching up on each other's lives. We also ate as much fried corn and fried green tomatoes as we could hold. The time went more quickly than we wanted, and then it was time to return to the farm. We said tearful goodbyes.

After we returned from seeing Pauline, Jab, Cordie and baby Willie left for California together. Now that I knew we would all go to California eventually, I didn't cry.

Cordie stayed in California with Jab for a year, until '45, and then she came back to Arkansas. She had found government housing for the family, a four-bedroom apartment in Berkeley, California. In the same building in Oakland where Cousin Minner lived they'd also found a small apartment for Paw and Ma.

While Jab and Cordie were gone for that year to California, we sharecropped with Ma and Paw, the last year of sharecropping we ever did. We lived on a place called Pickens' place. When the crop was ready, we got it up, cashed it in, settled all our debts, then moved from that place so the landowners wouldn't know we were actually leaving for California.

We moved on to Cousin Nathan's place by the railroad track close to town. He had his own property. We didn't know how he got it, but he had it.

I suspected he might have won it in a poker game. Cousin Nathan was as big as Paw, something over six foot three, and was always jolly. Every time he came around, he would tell us a joke, play with or tease us. He was our grandmother's cousin.

We stayed with Cousin Nathan from late December of 1944 to June of 1945. He had an extra house on his place for us. We had two or three cows we milked, some chickens, and we worked around Nathan's place with him, caring for his crops. Nathan had been married, but he had no children, and I never knew what had happened to his wife.

I was scared of snakes. When it would rain hard, there was a part of the street that would flood, and the snakes would climb up on the fence posts or lay out on the fence. To kill them, my brothers would pour kerosene on them. They would fall off in the water, and I would think they were going for my bare feet. I'd take off running. Every time Cousin Nathan came by he would tease me. "Seen any snakes lately, son?"

We now had six boys, Albert, John, St Clair Jr., Charlie, Eston and Willie, plus one girl. Dot was the only girl. Cordie came back to Arkansas with baby Willie to help us all get ready to move to California in the summer of 1945. We left our cows and chickens with Nathan when we went to California. We also left my grandmother's mother, Josephine Hill, the one who'd gotten Dot and me so sick chewing our first tobacco, with Nathan when we moved to California.

Chapter Four

Reunited by the Bay

The great migration day finally came in June of 1945. Since Cousin Nathan's place lay close to town, and the railroad ran near his house, Dot and I had watched trains rumble by many a day. We'd seen the people talking or eating dinner through the windows at night. Now we were going to ride a train ourselves – a three-day journey to California. We were excited!

Dot went through her clothes a dozen times. "I think these shorts better stay in Arkansas," she said, holding them up to the light. "Too many holes in the behind." Eventually, she got her battered suitcase packed.

When the train pulled into Dumas, I trembled at the tremendous rumble that shook my bones, even through the platform. We scrambled aboard and made our way toward the back. The train rules reminded me of the bus.

Colored folks could only sit in the last two coaches of the train. Nevertheless, ten excited colored folks, three adults and seven kids, boarded that train. My grandmother had carefully prepared individual lunch bags with pork chops and fried chicken as well as other good food, plus a large box of refills. She knew we couldn't purchase food from the dining car because of racial segregation, nor could we afford it.

Those two rear coaches offered standing-room only. Dot and I sat on our luggage. My grandmother and grandfather were offered seats, not cushioned seats, but seats nevertheless, by other colored folks who respected their age. The rest of our family stood. The crowded conditions didn't diminish our excitement, though. Dot talked faster than the train could move, giving a running description to all who were looking at the same thing she saw outside the train windows.

The train rolled from Dumas to Pine Bluff, from Pine Bluff to Little Rock.

The rear coaches were overcrowded because in June 1945 World War II in Europe had just ended. A lot of soldiers traveled home on the trains. Even though colored soldiers had served their country, paid for our freedom, the Jim Crow laws kept them from sitting where they wanted on the train. Many other colored people on the train were migrating out of the South to the north and west to get jobs. The last two cars were packed full. People were standing up, yet the rest of the train rolled along nearly empty!

The hot, humid, crowded conditions didn't improve until the train reached St. Louis, Missouri. When the train pulled into the station at St. Louis, the red caps, who were all colored, let us know we had arrived in a northern state and could move to any spot in the train we wanted. Adults and children joyously spread out all through that train, shoving our luggage into the luggage racks.

As we traveled further from home, Dot began to say, "Look at that thing, Charlie. What is it?"

I looked. "It's a truck," I answered, not really knowing, but wanting an answer.

Cordie looked out to see what Dot was asking about. "It's a tractor," she said. "They use it like they use a mule."

Instead of the mules, horses and wagons we'd been used to in Arkansas, we saw tractors, cars, bicycles, motorcycles and vehicles we didn't even know the names of. It seemed as though we were witnessing two different countries! When the train crossed the Mississippi River, it stopped on a trestle. We had never seen anything like this huge rolling body of muddy water.

In our much more comfortable circumstances we rode over the prairies, through the tunnels and over the sky-touching mountains that are the Rockies down into the desert to Salt Lake City. We'd never seen mountains before, and now, seeing a desert with this city in it was a whole new world to us.

Dot shouted, "Will ya'll just take a look at them lights all over the place! I ain't nevah seen so many lights.

Look at all the lights. What make them burn? What are those, Mama? They're not kerosene lamps. Ain't got a fire in there."

"They're electric lights, Dorothy Lee," Mama replied. Dot glued her face to the window.

We'd heard about great cities before, and had even seen one on this trip, St. Louis, but never one in the middle of a barren desert, with our own eyes. When the train crossed the Great Salt Lake, it stopped again, right in the middle. The train personnel told the passengers about the lake and gave an explanation of their surroundings. They also gave us little sacks of salt. Dot and I put our index fingers to our tongues and then touched the salt, returning it to our tongues, enjoying the twang of bitter taste immensely. The trip excited us to the point we hated to go to sleep when it got dark. Night irritated us because we couldn't see the country we were traveling through anymore.

I felt sure we'd passed another mountain range because in addition to the train's normal chugging, the train swayed first one way then another the night after we left Salt Lake

City. Sure enough, by the time the sun was up, we were already headed down through foothills into the San Joaquin Valley of California, and I could only see the Sierra Nevada behind us. The fact that we had made California excited Dot and me so much that we could hardly contain ourselves.

Dot asked, "Mama, is this it?" at every town we passed.

When the train finally pulled into Oakland, California, we saw Jab waiting on the platform outside the train windows waiting to pick us up. I had never seen him look so good. He wore a suit, a tie and a felt hat. We couldn't get off the train fast enough.

"Daddy!" we screamed and flew into his arms. We hugged and hugged until Jab finally put the little ones down, and said, "I expect we'd better let Cousin Minner get Grandma, Grandpa and Albert to where they can rest."

Albert was going to live with Grandma and Grandpa because he had a close relationship with them.

Jab drove the rest of the family up to Berkeley in a four-door 1936 Chrysler to their new apartment. The nine of us shared four-bedroom Apartment C, upstairs in the projects at 1021 10th Street. We first traveled up the Bayshore Highway, where to our amazement, three lanes of cars drove in the same direction. Jab purposely turned the opposite direction from our apartment first. Driving along Shattuck Avenue, I first saw San Francisco Bay sparkling in the sunlight. "I never saw so much water in my life!" I blurted.

Dad laughed. "That's only the Bay, son. The ocean is water as far as you can see, all the way to where the water meets the sky. I'll take you over and show you one of these days."

After our glimpse of the Bay, Jab drove us up to our Berkeley apartment. I was nine years old then, had seen a few tall buildings, but I couldn't believe this huge building was to be our home.

The buildings in what we came to know as "the projects" were two stories high. Once we climbed the stairs I murmured, "Good gracious! This is a big place," rambling from room to room.

Our apartment had electric lights, indoor plumbing and water that came right out of the faucet! No pumping, water just came out! All the walls were painted, inside and out. Besides that, there were no animals to care for.

The toilet had a white bowl at the top and a white bowl at the bottom where we did our business. A person pulled the chain and it all disappeared. I didn't know how it worked or where it went, but I thought, *No more runs to the outhouse in the snow for me.* I stood around and played with the toilet and experimented with it just for the novelty.

"We have died and gone to Heaven," Dot exclaimed.

Life among the tall concrete buildings in Berkeley wasn't segregated, either.

As a matter of fact, before we came to California, our family hadn't known any Mexicans, Filipinos, or any other nationality of folks. Dot and I hadn't even known they existed. In Berkeley we met people from all over the world who had come to the United States to make a home.

Seven of us went to Carnissas Village, a little elementary school. On school days we traded our overalls for Levis, V-neck T-shirts and sometimes sweaters. No more bare feet, now we had tennis shoes. On Saturdays we wore khakis starched so stiff they could stand by themselves

I felt extremely afraid of white girls because of what Jab and Paw had taught me about never talking to a girl with white skin. I knew that killing a black boy who looked at a white girl in the South was not a punishable offense. Because of that, I had always avoided speaking to, touching or even looking at a white girl. Then at Carnissas Elementary they sat me behind a little girl who was kind of pudgy with rosy cheeks, and white.

"Hi, she said. "My name's Sally. I'm pretty good at math, and if you need help with your work, I'll help you."

I kept my eyes on my desk.

"Well, you could be a little friendlier," she said.

I stared at the letter someone had carved in the wood top of my desk, praying the teacher wasn't calling someone to come and get me.

To my horror, Sally touched my hair. She felt it. Why did she think she could just touch someone's hair! My heart beat so hard, I thought I'd die before anyone had time to kill me.

"Miss Nelson, this new boy won't talk to me. Is he deaf?"

I peeked up to see what was going to happen. The teacher glanced back at me, and said, "It's not time to talk now anyway, Sally. Give Charlie some time to get acquainted."

They could have given Charlie the rest of my life and I'd never have talked to that little white girl. Days went by and she would try to get me to do my work, but I would just look at my desk.

I couldn't talk to her. I thought, *if I'm going to be killed, it isn't going to be because of Sally.*

Finally, the teacher, also white, came by my house trying to find out why I wouldn't talk to the little girl.

Mom explained, "Charlie is probably shy of white girls because of the hangings in the South."

After that the teacher moved me to a spot in the corner where I could study more easily. Now I sat behind a boy.

The war years were prosperous times for black people, kids as well as adults. We children could sell anything, tires, pop bottles or any kind of glass, even milk bottles. That's how we got money. If someone threw away an old tire casing, we could get one dollar for it, a lot of money then. Candy bars were two for a nickel. The most expensive candy bar we could find cost a nickel. Jab would give us a quarter every week for allowance. With that quarter, I could go to the movies, buy bubblegum and two candy bars or one candy bar and a bag of popcorn. Owning a quarter was tall cotton to me. Having one dollar in my pocket made me feel rich! We had money. We did things. We went places and had a lot fun. My brothers and I learned to ride the streetcars, get transfers, and get from Berkeley to Oakland and back.

The first year we were in California, I got a pair of roller skates for Christmas. I learned how to roller skate, and I could skate all the way from 10th Street in Berkeley to the Fox Theatre in Oakland. I also got a bicycle, just as Jab had hoped I would.

People used a place right out of Oakland, now called Emeryville, as a huge garbage dump. When anyone came close to Oakland, they could smell the terrible smell where everyone dumped their garbage in the bay. My brothers and I would walk all the way over there and brave the smell to find bottles, rubber tires and whatever else we could find. Then we'd sell our loot and use the money to go to the movies.

We lived in Berkeley for three years. I went through the fourth, fifth and sixth grades there, and the time changed my life.

I became Californiaized. None of the family, except Grandmother Lucinda, went to church anymore. Grandmother Lucinda asked where she could find the Baptist church no matter where we lived. The rest of us focused on making ends meet, how to make the dollar.

As time went by, Jab joined the Masons. Cordie took up smoking ready-rolled Lucky Strikes because she thought it cool.

On one particular day, Jun, our nickname for St. Clair Jr., said, "Man, I'd like to go to the movies." "Have you got any allowance left?" Dad asked. "None, but I'd still like to go. Maybe we could go sell somethin'."

"Have you cleaned your room?" Mom asked.

"Why don't you stay out of this," Jun sassed. We had always said, "Yes, ma'am" or "No, sir" to our parents in Arkansas. Now that we lived in Berkeley, we'd heard the rebellious way other kids talked to their parents, and I realized Jun was trying it out at home.

The tone of Dad's voice warned us all. "What did you say?" he asked sharply.

"No, ma'am," Jun answered. "I'll go do it right now." No sir and yes ma'am would stay part of our lives, at least at home. We weren't *that* Californiaized.

The war finally ended, and all the soldiers were coming home. Curfews and blackouts were still in effect when planes flew over, and for me, the blackouts meant fun. My brothers and I jumped out the window of our two-story bedroom and dropped to the lawn. We ran through the city and helped ourselves to little things we wanted – like soda pop. We were learning to steal.

A Canada Dry distribution warehouse with a ten-foot wall operated near our home, and we boys all loved ginger ale. During more than one blackout we scaled the wall and stole a case of twelve bottles. First we drank the ginger ale, then we sold the bottles for $.60. It only cost $.14 to go to the movies, but at that point we only had enough money for four guys.

Since usually two or three brothers as well as some friends wanted to go, we'd take the case of bottles over to the store and sell it the first time for $.60. The clerk would take the bottles out to a little bin in the back. Then we'd go out there as many times as we needed, take the bottles out of the bin and sell them two or three times to the same guy.

That way, we could all go to the movies, and have some popcorn or whatever, as well. John, our oldest brother, could stay out late because he was 16, and he left the door open so the rest of us could sneak back into the apartment. Living in Berkeley, we learned how to do sneaky things like that.

My brothers and I also learned to fight and adapted to the gang-type life quickly. Once we found out what gangs were, we realized we'd actually brought our own gang to town. Whether we were fighting one kid or fifteen, all six of us were in the fight. We were right out of Arkansas, and tough because of the hard labor we'd done in the fields.

Nobody wanted to mess with the Crane boys because no one else had that many brothers. We were feared wherever we went. It took a while for us to realize the power of our numbers, but once we did we used it to our advantage.

I joined Mom in learning to smoke, too. She didn't mind. She wasn't that much older than her children, and felt she related to us, even in smoking.

However, one day I stood behind the apartment building with some other guys smoking and shooting the breeze. Dad came up the walk returning from the shipyard and heard us. He said nothing until he appeared at the corner of our apartment building and looked directly at me. "Charlie, come with me," he ordered.

As we headed up the stairs, I wished I had time to pad my pants. "I'm going to have to whip you, because I've told you before that smoking is only for grownups, not for you. You've got to listen to me, boy. You're not old enough to be smoking."

Dad brought out the belt and laid into me, but it didn't stop me from smoking. I felt tough, and taking the beating was proof. I did try to hide my smoking after that, though, because each time Dad caught me again, I suffered another whipping.

Even policemen on the beat who saw us Crane boys out after curfew left us alone. One of the funniest stories told by the kids on the streets in Berkeley was about the time we outran a rookie who'd been a track star in high school. We had better sense than to let our parents know what we were doing on the street, though.

During this time Mom gave birth to another daughter, Wilma, whom the family called Beanie.

Image OF A Black Father

By 1948 the war boom had ended. Many shipyards were closing because the war had ended three years before, and what jobs left were taken by returning soldiers. Many Negro people had migrated from the South because of these great jobs. Thousands of us who'd come from Arkansas, Louisiana, Oklahoma and Texas – all the southern states, were now laid off, displaced.

We wanted to do something other than farm someone else's land, but though the Depression of the '30s had ended for white people, this was the Depression for Negro people.

To solve the "Negro problem," President Truman started a relief program using subsidized food to keep people from starving. This "temporary" program is what we call welfare today.

However, any home that had an able-bodied man in it couldn't get the subsidized food. The men losing their jobs were told that if they would go back to the farmland and establish themselves, the government would take care of their families. The welfare people came to the houses of people around our apartment checking to make sure no able-bodied men were around.

In Dad's case, especially because he only had a third grade education, the only thing he could do was farm. When he lost his job at Alameda Naval Shipyard, he got severance pay that would give him money to go back to Arkansas and get set up in sharecropping again. Not my dad. He said, "Forget it."

He wouldn't leave his family again, and he never took handouts. That's what made him my hero. He was always there for us, and he lived with integrity. Jab said, "We'll figure out something to do." I thought, *Dad doesn't know it, but if we stay in Berkeley, my brothers and I may end up in prison or somewhere worse.* Nevertheless, we'd carved our place, and hoped to stay. However, Dad didn't keep his family by the Bay.

Chapter Five

Grapes of Wrath

In 1948 Dad asked around Berkeley to find out whether farmers grew cotton anywhere in California. Someone told him people farmed cotton in the San Joaquin Valley, down around Merced County. Shortly after that, Dad made a trip down J152, a little highway on the way between Merced and Dos Palos. Blink-your-eyes-and-you-miss-it towns that consisted mostly of grocery stores dotted this road lined with dust and weeds. Jab met a black man named Tim Williams in El Nida. This town had a grocery store, as well as a gas station and a mail drop for people who lived in the area. Mr. Williams owned 20 acres where he grew peaches, watermelons and other fruit. He sold the sweetest 100-pound watermelons found anywhere, as well as other produce, to the stores in Merced and around the county.

Mr. Williams told Jab he would help him find a place large enough for our family if Dad wanted to move to that area to pick cotton.

They struck a deal, and Dad returned to Berkeley saying, "We're moving to Merced County."

None of the family felt excited about this move because we wanted to stay with the friends we'd made and the life we'd come to enjoy. However, we all wanted to stay together, so we planned the move. Mr. Williams had a two-and-a-half-ton Chevrolet truck he used hauling his fruit. He offered to let our family use it to move down to Dos Palos. We loaded most of the children in our car, with Grandma Lucinda and Paw, who drove. Dad drove Mr. Williams' truck with Mom in the cab with him, and Albert, John, Jun and I rode in the back of the truck with all our furniture and clothes. We left the city by the bay behind and headed to the San Joaquin Valley.

As I watched San Francisco Bay disappear behind us, I thought of all the fun the family had playing in the Pacific Ocean, riding the ferry across to San Francisco, roller skating and bicycling, going to the movies, all of it. Mom and Dad were up in the cab where I didn't think they could hear me, so I said to John, who sat next to me, "I'd still rather stay in Berkeley."

John replied softly, but with resentment in his eyes, "We come out of a bitter situation in Arkansas, I remember. We passed into the Promised Land in Berkeley. Now Dad's doin' the same as takin' us back to Arkansas."

Albert turned his face toward the highway behind them and added, "I ain't pickin' no cotton!"

We topped the Altamont Pass and looked over into the sun-scorched valley. "I think we been kicked out in the desert," Jun murmured. But the yellowed grass and the blazing sun weren't the worst of it.

When we drove into the place called Baker's Camp where we would live in the summer of the year I turned 12 we were shocked. I noticed our grandmother's face. Big tears rolled from her eyes. First of all, she'd made good friends at her Baptist church in Oakland; second, she was getting too old for this trucking all over the place; and third, Baker's Camp

Image OF A Black Father

was a nomad tent city! I would have cried too, if I hadn't wanted to keep up my tough image.

We ended up living in four old 25-pointed Army tents that rolled up on the side to get air. It was the same type of housing we'd had in Arkansas, no electricity, no running water, and outdoor toilets, but these tents didn't have cracks in the walls because they didn't even have walls.

On the first night, Dot murmured, "I think I'm goin' to hate it here."

Every farmer who had any land at all had set up a camp for the migrant people who came to work on his ranch.

Our family moved to Baker's Camp to pick fruits and vegetables, and then cotton for the season, about nine months. I finally learned how to do farm labor work. I picked those sharp cotton bolls with bare hands, and learned to use Vaseline on the wounds just like the rest of my family. I was no longer a houseboy. To make $10 I had to pick 330 pounds of cotton. However, I didn't get all of that $10. Dad had a sharecropping arrangement with us boys. We kept half of what we made, the rest went to the family. With our half we had to buy our school clothes and whatever else we wanted other than food.

Like back in Arkansas, only Negro people who did field work seasonally populated the camps. We irrigated, hauled hay, or whatever the farmer who owned the camp needed us to do. We enjoyed no social life except if we took time from working to go into town, maybe to church. We children went to school, and had to make new friends.

However, Dad did organize one picnic for everyone in our camp. "Ya'll pile in the cars," he called to the bunch of boys all standing first on one foot and then on the other waiting for the picnic to start. In our minds we could already smell that barbecue and feel the tug of those fish on our lines. The camp folks owned only two cars, one other man's and Dad's '41 Ford. We filled them both up with boys. Jab planned to take all us boys down first so we could swim while he brought the women, girls and all their cooking paraphernalia.

The two cars made the trip and dropped their cargo off on the San Joaquin River. As we looked out over the rolling water a big long board stuck on a tree protruding from the bank caught our eyes. "We can float everybody across the river on this board," one of us yelled. Two boys went across at a time, and one of them would bring the board back. The older boys swam across first.

I didn't know how to swim and neither did my friend, Agee Lee, whose real name was Adrian. He was a year younger than me. As we held back on the bank waiting for the older boys to go, I observed, "This is a pretty big river."

"Yeah, my knees are knocking some," Agee responded. When John came back with the board, I got on and began to paddle across. In the middle, the current began to move us downriver, but we paddled with all our might and made the other side. A boy named Alphinas brought the board back, and this time Agee Lee got on and they started across again.

Right in the middle of the river the board flipped somehow and floated away. Alphinas had no time to worry about why the board flipped, because as soon as Agee Lee lost it, he began to panic. He thrashed about, trying to grab Alphinas and hollering for help. River water splashed into his mouth as he cried, "Help! Somebody come get me!" When Alphinas finally got away from Agee Lee, he was nearly drowned himself.

Agee Lee's brother, Alton, who couldn't swim either, yelled, "Go get him!"

My two older brothers, Albert and John, could swim, and jumped in to try to save Agee Lee. I could only stand helplessly on the side of the river and watch.

Not thinking of trying to hold something out to him, John and Albert tried to save Agee Lee with their hands. In his panic, he nearly drowned all three of them. He grabbed one and then another, pushing them under the water trying to crawl on their backs.

My brother, John, was the last one to have him. The two of them sank, wrestling, below the water. The rest of us on shore watched the water boil above them for what seemed like five minutes. Finally, John came up without Agee Lee. We had to pull him out, he had become so exhausted. Agee Lee didn't come out. We didn't see him anymore. We looked all along the river as far as we could go until we heard the cars coming back.

When Dad and the other man driving arrived with the women, we told them what had happened. Agee Lee's mother began to cry and scream, and the other women cried with her.

Most of the grownups combed the banks of the river again while a few others went to call for help.

Two hours later the fire department came and dragged the river with a seine. They found Agee Lee about a mile downstream. When his mother heard, she slumped to the ground and wailed. I couldn't believe I had stood there on the bank, unable to swim, watching my friend drown, yelling for help. I felt empty and dark.

Agee Lee's family was so grieved they packed up and moved back to Louisiana.

For a long time after that, Dad felt it was all his fault because he'd taken the boys to the river without adults to watch them. He grieved about it. He never showed grief with tears, but anyone could see the pain in his face. There were no more picnics on the river.

However, in El Nida we children no longer stole, outran policemen or sneaked out at night.

We were too far out in the country to get into the kind of trouble we had started enjoying in Berkeley.

Bicycling down the road only took us further down the road. There simply wasn't any trouble to get into.

As we moved from farm to farm, Dad worked for one man named Mr. Blitz, who raised sheep as well as cotton and other crops. Dot and I attended a school called Alamo while we lived there. It was rough. The children of the people we worked for would tease us about what we had for lunch, what we were wearing, even our hair. They didn't like anything about the Crane kids. I ate by myself.

My teacher, Miss Charlotte Warner, always comforted me when the kids would criticize me. I never had a fight at Alamo, maybe because my older brothers wouldn't go to school, so I didn't have them to back me up, or maybe because of Miss Warner. Dot was there, but the rest would have had to get on a bus to go to junior high. They worked instead of attending school because there wasn't a mandatory education law then. However, Mom and Dad made Dot and me go.

That winter, at Mr. Blitz's place, one of the jobs was to cut off the sheep's tails and then cauterize them to keep the fly problem down. Then they were dipped in sheep dip. Dad and the white foreman, Shorty, had a fire going one day to work on the sheep.

My younger brother, Eston, who was five or six years old by then, went with them so he could play with the lambs. Dad had gone up to the house to get something, and Shorty worked with the sheep in the field. Eston took a five-gallon can and poured gas on the fire. When he did, the can blew up and fire went everywhere. Eston, ablaze, ran down the road yelling for Shorty.

"Catch me, Shorty! Catch me, Shorty!" Eston yelled.

Shorty, was a little guy and older, but he could run. "Oh my God, oh my God," he yelled when he saw what had happened. He caught Eston and rolled him in a pool of water nearby. The boy sobbed and so did Shorty.

Dad heard the yelling and came running from the house. The fire had cooked Eston. When Jab peeled his pants back, skin came with them. Eston screamed.

When he settled down, he said, "Take me out of this water, Daddy, I'm cold." They wrapped him in a blanket and drove him into town to the doctor. Shorty sat right down by the pond and cried for a long time. I stood there patting him on the back. Finally, when his shoulders stopped heaving, I said, "Shorty, if you hadn't caught Eston, he would have died."

It didn't take much time at all, though, before Eston was back out playing. He healed fast.

Mom also had four more children during this time. First came Shirley, then Geraldine, then Ray and finally, Katherine. All these new members of the family were girls, except Ray. I thought it funny that in Arkansas Cordie had all boys and one girl, and now in California she'd had all girls and one boy.

After that, our family moved into Dos Palos to pick peaches and do whatever other work we could find. Now we had a house with electric lights, but we still had to drive into town to get water. The water in that flat plain has never been good for drinking, only good for growing plants. Maybe it's because grease weed grows there, or maybe the alkaline soil. Whatever the reasons, we had to drive to town to get water. In Dos Palos I now learned planing and listing the furrows.

Dos Palos offered much more social life than El Nida had, too. We had a teenage joint, a place for the kids to go, run by my cousin, Lovie. Her husband had been killed in a car wreck. She started this place in a two-story building where she lived upstairs, and made her living selling the kids sandwiches and sodas downstairs. She had a jukebox and a little Formica counter, and all the rest was dance floor. The jukebox only cost five cents to play a record. The kids would go every Friday and Saturday night. My older brothers and I, except for Jun, spent a lot of time there chasing girls.

Jun, who was two years older than I was, was paralyzed in 1952 through surgery caused by what was believed to have been a brain tumor. The surgery had rendered his left arm and foot immobile, so he wasn't able to work, dance or much of anything, anymore.

My grandmother, in contrast to us kids, had found another church and went every Sunday. She tried to encourage us to sing in the choir and perform in church plays. I did, every once in a while. However, I mostly drank white port wine mixed with lemon juice and danced at Lovie's all night.

The majority of people in Dos Palos had moved from the cotton fields of Oklahoma to the cotton fields of Dos Palos. It seemed like a small southern town, where they worked hard all week, and then partied all weekend. A lot of men and women would go out with other people's husbands or wives. Mom and Dad didn't behave that way, but a lot of others did. Married men and single men went out, chased women and drank every weekend. Then when they'd get caught, they'd have to fight.

Everybody knew everybody and all the carousing they did, but they did it anyway. Motown had started up, with the Platters and the Drifters and all the big time bands, and the young people were having fun, too. Dos Palos was a wild place in the '50s. Many of the Crane children's teen years saw that environment. I began to make choices about living that later got me into trouble.

One weekday when I was about 14, Dad and I were working together. Dad sat down to rest and let me drive the tractor he'd been plowing the field with. John Harmon, the owner, came by about then and seeing what a good job I was doing, said, "How'd you like a job?"

I snapped up the offer, and worked for John Harmon off and on the whole time we lived in Dos Palos. However, whatever I made, the family still claimed half. During this time, I would work for two or three months and then take off to Los Angeles or somewhere else trying to find a better life. Not finding one, I'd return to Dos Palos and go back to work for John.

Every time I came back, Dad said, "This kind of work won't take you through life. You have to go on to something else. Finish school. You need that diploma." Dad didn't know what else I had to learn, because he never got that far. Nevertheless, he continued to encourage me to raise my sights.

Chapter Six

All Men Art Not Equal

"Dad, I want to get away from the cotton fields, the farms. I think I can make a career of the Army, like John has. I want to enlist," I told him one day in early 1954. The Korean War was in progress, and I was about to graduate from high school.

Dad stopped hoeing and wiped his forehead with his handkerchief. "That so," he said more than asked. "I believe it would be a good choice for you, Charlie. Get away from drinkin' wine and hangin' out with your friends on Saturday nights." He returned to the hoeing. "If you're going to be a soldier, be the best soldier you can be," he added. "I think you should do it. Go ahead."

The government draft enlisted me for two years. My papers were drawn to draft me on my eighteenth birthday in March, but I didn't enter the military until July 21, so I could graduate.

I told Mom in June because I knew she wouldn't like the idea. "Mom, I'm going to join the Army," I said one day as she stirred the lunch we'd have.

"No, you're not," she replied, without looking up.

"I've already done it, Mom, because I don't want to pick and irrigate cotton my whole life. The draft notice is here, see?"

I handed her the paper.

"Charlie, I don't want you to go. They've got John. What do they need you for!"

"I'm planning to make a career of it, Mom. It'll be a good opportunity for me."

"If you don't get killed. Did you think of that?"

"I could get killed crossing the street."

"Maybe so, but less opportunity. I'm not giving this my blessing, Charlie." "OK, Mama."

She turned and looked up at me. "Dad blame it, you've always been a hard head," she said and hugged me.

Then I knew it would be all right. Not that she would give me her blessing, but it would be all right between us.

I took sixteen weeks of basic training at Fort Ord, California among the sand dunes on the Pacific Ocean at Monterey Bay. The military had integrated six years prior to my enlistment, and I took the training with the white soldiers, ate with them and slept in the same barracks.

I felt proud to wear my new uniform because it said I was a first-class citizen. I was in top physical condition from throwing boxes of tomatoes and pitching watermelons on trucks in Dos Palos as well as boxing in high school. I still boxed on Friday nights. As I looked forward to becoming a paratrooper like John, I enjoyed the rifle range, the marching, and learning the basic commands and general orders, eleven of them. My mind worked well, being right out of high school, and I could rattle orders off just like that.

Then I got a letter from John, who now served in Korea. "Don't be a paratrooper," John wrote.

"It's the worst job in the military."

I went to my company commander and told him I had changed my mind about becoming a paratrooper. The commander sent me through eight more weeks of advanced training, at the end of which came an aptitude test. I filled mine out, starting with my name, rank, Private B1, and serial number US56139391. The next thing to note was race. At that time African Americans were called Negroes. I came to believe that when a person marked "Negro," the test automatically went into a separate basket, because all the Negroes in my platoon came back qualified to be cooks or truck drivers. Two choices. Other people were clerk typists, electrical engineers, or some other skilled job, but Negroes were drivers or cooks.

John had served as a cook down in Fort Benning, Georgia, but I had cooked through my entire childhood. I didn't want to cook *anything*. I went out to the motor pool and passed a test for a military driver's license. Because I boxed on the fort boxing team, the commander wanted to give me an easy job. He liked me.

He made me his company driver. I drove him around the post and ran errands for him in a little Jeep.

However, one day I returned from picking up shipping orders at the company headquarters, and the commander said, "Charlie, I'm sorry to tell you this, but your platoon just shipped out to Camp Kilman, New Jersey, and you missed the plane."

I replied, "OK, great. I didn't want to go anyway. I've been hoping they were going to keep me right here in Fort Ord. I like the beach pretty well."

"No, we're going to put you on a hop," the commander responded. "We have a seat on a plane that's going to Fort Knox, Kentucky. I'll send a pass that says you go from there to Camp Kilman."

This hop was a set up where I went down to the airport and waited for the next available plane. I only had to wait for about an hour.

They put me on with a group of soldiers going to typing school. They all would become clerk-typists, and every single one was white.

Shortly after I climbed on the old prop job plane, I noticed a peculiar smell. We were up over Los Angeles when the red "fasten your seatbelt" light came on. Smoke began to come from the cockpit. Shortly after that, a flight attendant came down the aisle and said, "Everything's OK, some wires in the heating system caught fire, but we were able to put it out. However, I have to tell you, the heating system doesn't work." The rest of that trip, they froze.

The plane landed in Memphis, Tennessee for breakfast. We jumped off the plane into a field, cold to the bone. My feet were so cold they were numb. We jumped into two feet of snow on the ground, and all raced for the restaurant to get a cup of coffee and warm up. It was December 19, 1954.

The proprietor let the 55 clerk-typists go in to eat, but he stopped me at the door. I didn't realize what was happening at first. We'd been in California for a long time.

Then the proprietor said, "You can't eat in here. We don't serve coloreds. Go on around to the back."

I stood stunned. I felt two inches tall. Rejected. I didn't belong in this bitter world by myself. I only belonged to my family, who were far away, back in California. I must have stood dumbly in the doorway too long.

The proprietor yelled, "You go on around the back there, and get something to eat!"

"No, I don't ..." I tried to tell him I didn't want to eat.

"I said go around the back! We have a place back there for you. We have 56 meal tickets and we're going to feed 56 soldiers."

"I'll just get back on the airplane."

"Go around the back. NOW!"

I felt so humiliated I finally moved around to the back, because I was afraid that if I didn't, the proprietor would

Image OF A Black Father

have me arrested. The little room, about 10 by 10, had a table with a red-and-white checkered tablecloth on it.

It looked clean, but it seemed ugly to me because I'd been singled out again. I was hungry as well as cold, so I ate a good breakfast. While I ate, I decided, *I wear the same uniform those guys wear, and I can't even eat with the people I may die for. I belong to the federal government, I'm the property of the U.S. Army, and I'm going to lay my life down for my country, but I can't even eat in a restaurant. I'll not try to please this government or this system ever again. My loyalty to the U.S. is over. I'll get through this, and then I'm going back to my family.*

I stayed five days in Camp Kilman. Then I shipped out to Panama. No one I knew went with me; no one I'd served with at Ford Ord. I went alone. Maybe they sent me to the Canal Zone because I'd been on the boxing team. While I served there I tried out for the Olympic team, but didn't make it. I served for eighteen months, growing from a little farm boy to a Class A soldier, honorably discharged a corporal.

I arrived back in Dos Palos a bitter man because my country had denied me the military career I'd imagined. Again, I went out to see John Harmon.

"Oh, hi," John said, as if I'd never left. My farm labor days were right there waiting for me. I thought now and then about going back to the military, but I worried I'd experience the same prejudice I had before but this time not be able to hold my temper.

Since I had gained the right to three years of schooling through my time in the service, I went to Los Angeles to barber college. However, as usual I couldn't find a job, and nearly starved to death. I came back to Dos Palos again and worked the fields. Each time I had enough money, I'd take off looking for a job in the city, Palo Alto, Redwood City, anywhere. I wanted something that would last, something permanent. I didn't want to do farm labor like Jab did. After all, Jab only did it because he had to.

Every weekend I went back to my old lifestyle. I'd get drunk, dance, fight, and get put in jail.

I hated white people, and wouldn't go around them unless I had to. When I did, I'd end up in fights with them. These fights weren't personal, they resulted from the way life had treated me. I had become discouraged with what being black meant.

Five times I went to jail for disturbing the peace. People got 90 days for disturbing the peace then. I always got arrested at the end of spring, starting into summer. During the winter the rains would wash out holes in the road. I worked on a road crew to fix these holes.

One good thing did happen to me during this time, though. I met a girl named Sherry. Sherry's parents were divorced. When she and I met, I was 20 and Sherry 14. Her mother wanted a big brother-type person to make friends with Sherry. She wasn't old enough to date. She didn't have many friends because her father had gone to prison. Her mother and my grandmother were friends, and her mother trusted me. I was probably one of the worst boys in Dos Palos, but her mother didn't know that.

To her, I seemed responsible, mature. I'd been in the military, and I could get a job in Dos Palos any time I wanted to.

I started taking Sherry out to movies or to go to the park, not like boyfriend/girlfriend, just friends. Until, when Sherry was in the twelfth grade, she asked me to take her to her senior prom. I had messed up with several girls by then, and really didn't want to take her.

"No, I'd just as soon you found someone else to go with," I told her.

"I want to go with you," she said, flatly.

I took her to the prom. I had no car, because my brother had totaled my car. So her mother let us use her car. That marked the turning point for me. Sherry came out dressed in an off-the-shoulder gown she had bought for the prom. She looked different and she talked different. I thought *Wow, I've been associating with a young lady. I thought she was a little girl. I better pay more attention to what's going on around here.* I started looking at her differently.

In June, after Sherry walked across the stage and received her diploma, I met her on the lawn. I knelt down, handed her an engagement ring as a graduation present, and said, "Will you marry me?"

"Yes," she answered. "But you need to know, I'm moving to Modesto to go to nursing school." Shortly after that, she and her family left Dos Palos for Modesto.

Chapter Seven

Following Sherry

With every day that passed, Sherry looked more attractive. Her dark, luminescent eyes held intelligence and character, and her calm ways beckoned me from my riotous weekends. I visited Modesto, a town of 30,000 people, much bigger than Dos Palos, with her family several times while they looked for a place to live.

We noticed that the colored quarters in Modesto were referred to as the "West Side." It was not a segregated area, but it was the only place black people could live. Churches, schools, grocery shopping and social clubs were conveniently located in that area to keep us in our place. Black folks could go anywhere in Modesto. There were no barriers or signs. However, many places had ways of making us feel uncomfortable. Most of the women who lived on the West Side of the city worked as nannies, housekeepers, maids, etc. The men worked as cooks, janitors, car washers, or in the fields.

While Sherry and her mother began preparations for their move, I lived with my grandmother in Dos Palos. Paw had died, and Lucinda felt content to be a widow. She'd had only one love in her life. Nevertheless, she was always glad to see me come back from my excursions to the cities because when I worked in Dos Palos and lived with her, I gave her money to help with expenses. In the evenings, she would have me read to her, always from the Bible. I drove a harvester at the time, but still went out on the weekends that I wasn't in Modesto. Her Bible didn't change my life much.

One Friday night in September of 1960 a friend, Arnold Lane, and I had gone out and drunk all night. We didn't even see our beds, going straight from the juke joint to work. Both of us worked on a team driving harvesters from one field to another down a highway. That day there were about ten in a row of huge International Harvesters that have a big blade on the front for cutting and gathering the wheat.

I drove second in line, and Arnold came right behind me. We stopped at a stop sign, but Arnold had gone to sleep. He ran his blade right into the back of my harvester.

The manager, Jack, came up and yelled at Arnold for breaking the blade on the harvester, "God damn it! You dumb son of a bitch, look what you've gone and done!" It took a lot of work and money to change one of those blades.

Arnold, groggy from all the drinking he and I had done, wobbled his head while Jack yelled at him.

I watched him wobble thinking Arnold looked like one of those dolls people put in the back windows of cars. I got tickled, and began to laugh. The more Arnold wobbled, the louder I laughed. I laughed louder and louder and harder and harder, and couldn't stop. Jack fired both of us. He threw our checks at us and yelled, "Leave and don't come back!" If we'd been sober, it would have been a degrading experience. As it was, we ambled off to Arnold's car and went to Lovie's.

Arnold had bought a brand new 1960 Dodge. The next Saturday evening he said, "I'm going to Oakland to see my brother. I'll be back on Sunday."

Seeing a free ride to see Sherry, I grinned and asked, "Why don't you drop me in Modesto, and then come back and pick me up." So we took off.

Arnold dropped me off in Modesto all right, but he never came back. He stayed with his brother in Oakland. I never went back to live in Dos Palos, either. I was free and had no obligations. I stayed in Modesto. Sherry's mother let me live with them for one week.

The sharecropper's son got up that Monday morning from the couch in the living room of Sherry's mother's house and walked downtown to look for a job. I needed a stable job because I had a mission. I'd slip a wedding ring on Sherry's finger before some college boy tried to cut in.

I owned only one change of clothes, and I was wearing them.

Walking for blocks and blocks down Paradise, clear up to Franklin, I crossed the railroad tracks and walked into the white part of town. I didn't know where to look for a job, not even where to find the employment office. When I got to 11th and L where Bill Hughes Used Cars stood then, I saw Bill Hughes and a few other guys out washing cars in their white shirts and ties.

Standing tall, I walked up to them and said, "You guys look like you need somebody to do this kind of work. You're not dressed for it."

Bill Hughes answered, "You know how to wash a car?"

"As good as you," I replied.

Bill Hughes handed me the bucket and the rag, and said, "OK, you're hired." At the end of the day, Bill paid me $10 and asked if I'd work on a permanent basis for $55 a week for a five and a half day week. I gladly took the job, and worked for Bill Hughes for three years for what amounted to $1.25 an hour. Hughes had another guy working for him named Harold Chase who detailed cars.

He shampooed the insides and steam cleaned the motors, washed the tires and painted them so cars looked like they were brand new. He taught me to detail.

I found room and board for $10 a week at the home of a couple named Roosevelt who'd moved from Madera to Modesto and lived on Marshall Street on the West Side.

A year later, on June 10, 1961, Sherry and I were married in Second Baptist Church on the West Side. Dad, Mom Grandmother Lucinda and all my brothers and sisters, except for Jun and John were there. By this time, I had bought a 1955 Ford on the installment plan. I'd also been frequenting weekly an auction on Seventh Street buying furnishings for our new home. I purchased a television, table and chairs and other things needed to set up housekeeping. Sherry was still going to nursing school, but beginning to realize it wasn't for her. We found an apartment in the projects on Robertson Road for $43 per month.

During this time Dr. Martin Luther King, Jr. preached his "free at last" sermons. I knew every black person in this country could relate to the nonviolence movement in the South. I had mixed emotions. Dr. King's "I have a dream" message made me cry. I tried not to, but the tears came anyway. I cried differently, in anger and bitterness when I watched the news on TV and saw the cruel treatment government officials gave the freedom marchers. When white people around me criticized the marchers or asked my opinion about it, I felt ashamed, because I was a fighter. I couldn't have handled nonviolence the way Dr. King did. I seldom commented on it because it made me fiercely angry.

If I had had to make a choice between Dr. King and Huey Newton and the Black Panthers, he'd have chosen the Panthers, a rebel group that organized to start riots and take things that didn't belong to them. They thought whites owed them. They wanted to change the ghetto.

Their motto, "Burn baby, burn," was based on the idea that if they burned the ghetto down, the whites, the government would have to build it back, and better. They knew they couldn't burn white homes. They were angry at the things that had happened to black people like the Cranes, at the government for the inequality, and they took out their anger in fire and blood in places like Watts in Los Angeles. I was in Modesto, not Los Angeles, and that probably kept me out of more trouble.

In 1962 I went to Bill Hughes and said, "I want to buy a house, but I want you to look at it first."

Bill looked a little puzzled, but said, "OK."

My car showed its age, so we got into one of Bill's cars and drove over to 426 Oak Street where a white man named Beech had a house for sale. The black people had started moving into that area, and he wanted to move out. The house cost $9500. He had wanted $11,000, but no one would give him that. The house had been on the market a while, so he had dropped the price to $9500.

When we got out of Bill's car in front of the house, I said, "Look at this house. Do you think this is a nice house?"

Bill answered, "Yeah, it's a nice house."

I continued, "It has two bedrooms, a bath, living room and a den with a fireplace that Beech built on. There's a large kitchen with a breakfast nook." Finally, I turned to Bill and said, "This is the house I want to buy."

Bill replied, "It's a good buy."

We drove back over to the car lot, and when we'd gotten almost to the office, I said, "Do you know why I haven't bought that house?"

"Why?"

"Because I don't have the money. I want to borrow the money from you."

Bill looked at me through squinted eyes and said, "How much do you need?"

I answered, "I need $250 to pay down."

"How are you going to pay me back?"

"I'm going to give you $10 a week out of my paycheck until it's paid back."

Bill didn't say anything. He walked into the office and said to his secretary, who was also his niece, "Give Charlie a check for $250 – and give him a $5 raise."

In 1962 Sherry and I also had our first child. We wanted children right away, and no one had told us we couldn't afford them. On May 9 Sherry delivered our eight pound, two ounce boy. Words couldn't express how proud I felt of Sherry. She had given Jab his first grandson to carry the Crane name, and she had made a real man out of me.

We named our son Kurry. This was the surname of my dad's favorite uncle, Charles Curry, with whom I shared a first name. Kurry's first words were Dad-da, of course, but he coined the name Cuppy for Sherry and stole her heart forever.

Our little family often drove to Dos Palos to show off Kurry to his grandparents and Jun. Jun made the best of his paralysis, but couldn't hold a job. He lived with Jab and Cordie.

The results of the Civil Rights movement became apparent in 1963. Up until that time only one black guy named Mel Williams worked for the City of Modesto. He pushed a little cart around collecting money from parking meters. The rest allowed to work in the city still worked on garbage trucks or as janitors, and such. The 14th Amendment basically provided job opportunities, fair housing and higher education for minorities. Sports, entertainment and politics started opening their doors to black people.

Though no company in Modesto had hired black people up to that time, except to shine shoes and such, Campbell Soup opened its doors. Nearly every able-bodied black person in Modesto went to work for them. Sherry and I went to work at Campbell Soup Company.

Sherry worked swing shift and I worked the other shifts so that one of us could be at home with the children. We began to have the means to buy things we wanted.

I still had the Dos Palos mentality. I wanted to work all week and go out on the weekends to dance and act crazy, even though I was married. I loved Sherry, but I didn't see anything wrong with catting around on Saturday night. Sherry wanted to stay home and have a family, and I wanted to go out and act crazy. Sherry would go to church on Sunday with her mother, and I would lie at home and sleep. This went on for a while.

Sherry next gave birth to our first daughter, Shawna, in September 1964. Shawna was beautiful. She didn't resemble Kurry at all. Actually, she looked like me. We considered our family complete, a boy for me and a girl for Sherry.

One morning I received a call from my mother, who rarely called anyone. Her voice trembled when she said, "Charlie, Jun's in Merced General Hospital. I left right away to see him.

During the half-hour trip, I tried praying, but I felt like what I said only drifted as far as the roof of the car and stopped.

The hospital folks ignored me, who knew which room Jun was in, and didn't need to ask directions. Jun lay alone in a cold room with breathing tubes and a heart monitor attached to him. His eyes were open, but he was in a coma. I talked to him for a long time. I didn't know if Jun could hear me, but I talked anyway.

"Jun, I remember all those times you rescued me in school," I told him. "Thank you. You never let me lose a battle with another kid. You were my hero. Hang on, Jun. I'm sorry I haven't been around since you've been hurt. Hang on, and I'll change. I'll be there, Jun," I begged.

Jun was 31, never married, and had no chance to experience being a father or the responsibility and joy of raising his own family. I wondered whether asking Jun to live was kind or unkind. Nevertheless, I talked until there was nothing left to say. Finally, I drove home.

The next day, Mom called again. The instant I heard her voice, I knew my brother was gone.

At the funeral, Mom cried hysterically. Dad spent his time consoling her. I never saw him cry, but the look on his face and the way his nose wrinkled revealed the hurt he felt in his heart. St. Clair Crane, Jr., his namesake, was the first of his 13 children to pass away.

When we had supper back at the house, Dad picked at his food and gave one-word answers when someone spoke to him.

To lighten the load of Jun's death, later that spring Sherry and I took Dad and Mom on a trip to Ohio, their first vacation since coming to Dos Palos. We went to visit Pauline, Dad's firstborn, in Toledo. It was a joyous reunion, and seemed to lift Jab and Cordie's spirits some.

When we got back to California, Jun's death had caused me to get more serious about my life. Sherry was really good at being a mother. She and I agreed she should be at home with the children. Therefore, I needed a career.

In 1966 I put in applications all over Modesto – U.S. Postal Service, Modesto Police Department, fire department. I went everywhere. Every application required an exam or some type of aptitude test. I took a two-hour exam for employment with Pacific Bell Telephone Company. There were no other minorities in the exam room. The administrator sat quietly in the front of the room.

When I finished the exam and handed it to her, she said, "I've observed you cheating during the test." She ripped my test papers and told me not to reapply.

Image OF A Black Father

I felt cheated for having no way to appeal her accusation, and angry that whitey was closing doors in my face again.

That afternoon, when I arrived at Campbell Soup Company, a friend told me United Parcel Service wanted minority applicants. He gave me the address on South Seventh Street and promised to meet me there at 8 a.m. the next day. I got there on time. The company gave me a short math quiz, a driving test in one of the package delivery cars, and made an appointment for a physical exam.

Before noon that same day they took measurements for my uniforms and asked if I could start work the following Monday. My friend never showed up. In fact, I never saw him again. When I began work for United Parcel Service, I was the first black man, because the government had to have a quota, to be hired by UPS in Modesto.

A few months later, Sherry, now at home with the kids, informed me that we were expecting our third child. I made up my mind that this one would be a Jun or Junior because girl or boy, its name was going to be Charlie Crane. In April of 1967, Sherry gave birth to an eight-pound girl whom, as a nod to her gender, we named Charlita.

Two of my younger brothers, Eston and Willie, had moved to Modesto before Charlita was born. They were a year apart and enjoyed social activities together. They both had served in the U.S. Army. Willie had been a military policeman in Saigon during the Vietnam War. Eston served in Anchorage, Alaska.

Eston had come to live with Sherrie and me first, and then Willie. They both had good jobs, and we three brothers continued our pattern of going out to do "social" drinking and act crazy on weekends. Eston and Willie were also both engaged and considering a double wedding ceremony. Eston's girlfriend lived in Fresno, about two hours south of Modesto. Willie's fiancé was in Modesto.

Image OF A Black Father

On Saturday, June 8, 1968, I was watching the funeral of Robert Kennedy on television when my friend, Curtis Fifer, came in. Curtis lived across the street. We decided to drive to Stockton for a haircut while we made plans for our Saturday night outing. There was no barber in Modesto.

Willie came in as we were about to leave and decided to go with us. As the three of them walked outside, Eston drove up. He looked tired and sleepy. It was obvious that he had been out all night drinking. He wanted to go with us, but we encouraged him to stay and get some sleep.

Before we could get him to bed, his girlfriend telephoned with an emergency. Her father had suffered a stroke. She wanted Eston to come to Fresno, 90 miles away. I removed the distributor wires from Eston's car to prevent him from driving in that condition.

"Charlie, please give me the distributor wires. I've got to help her," he pleaded.

"No. You're not in any shape to drive. Go get a couple of hours of sleep, and then go. You're not a doctor anyway, you can't help her."

"I'm OK. I can drive, Charlie. I can do this," Eston begged.

About that time the phone rang again. I answered, and it was Eston's girlfriend asking if Eston had left yet. I told her no, he was still there.

"Tell him my dad is already dead."

I felt sorry then, and handed Eston the wires. "Man, this is a mess. Please be careful, Eston. Drink a lot of coffee on the way."

Robert Kennedy's funeral was still on the television at the barbershop when the phone rang. It was Curtis' wife, who told him to drive Willie and me back home. Eston had had an accident. "I'll drive," Curtis said. We were driving my car, and Curtis' insistence told me it was bad.

Image OF A Black Father

I let Curtis drive my car. When we pulled up in front of my house, Sherry and some of our friends were in the front yard hugging and weeping. Eston was dead. It had happened on Highway 99 in Ceres, five miles south of our house. Eston had hit a post going 90 miles an hour. I knew Eston's accident could have been prevented. I should have driven Eston. I felt Eston needed to go to his fiancee, and I hadn't thought it through. I was to blame, since I had given the distributor wires back to my brother.

The highway patrol needed someone to identify Eston, and I went. My broken brother lay there, and my knees buckled at the sight of him. "Eston, Eston," I sobbed.

Now two of Dad's sons were gone. At Eston's funeral I said, "Dad, it was my fault. I had the wires, I should have kept them."

Dad's nose wrinkled. "Son, there was more to it than the wires," he answered. I wondered whether Jab's nose would ever come unwrinkled this time.

Losing Eston hurt the whole family. I knew I could have made a better decision, one that might have saved my brother's life and spared our pain. That made me hurt all the more. I wanted to change my life. I wanted to be a better person.

Chapter Eight

The Jesus Connection

In the days after Eston's death I ate, worked and slept because I had to, but a piece of my heart had died. I wanted someone to comfort me, to say the words that would take away the guilt of making the decision to give Eston back his distributor wires. None of my family could do that. The truth was that I made the wrong decision. No one could do anything. I had to live with it.

Dad never cried about Eston's death. He never cried about anything. Now and then his eyes would just stare into space. That was the only way I could tell he still hurt. One day he told me, "It was no one's fault. Eston knew he had drunk too much. He insisted. It was just his time." He looked me in the eye, trying hard to make me understand he didn't hold me responsible. "He had $10,000 worth of life insurance. Do you need anything?" he asked.

"No, Daddy. I don't want it." Despite Jab's forgiving attitude, every day something Eston and I would have done together, or talked about, renewed the pain in my heart.

Hoping to ease that pain, I thought back to the times I'd felt love and comfort back in Arkansas. The times I used to carry water to Dad as he plowed the fields, or walk barefoot on the hot dusty road with him, lay in the past where innocence used to live. I even remembered when I was a teenager in Dos Palos during the rainy season. There was no work, so Dad and I would gather wild mustard greens, seine the nearly empty canals for bass, carp, catfish and crawdads; and hunt jackrabbits together. Memories of those days in Dos Palos when I'd read the Bible to my grandmother as she rocked in her rocking chair even helped.

The small comfort of my memories left me still guilty, though. Finally, I decided to try church. I wanted to stop dancing, drinking and acting crazy.

I wanted to become the kind of person I needed to be. Sherry was already attending Second Baptist Church, and I joined her on a regular basis. That summer in 1968, I bought all the right church clothes. I joined the choir, hoping God would somehow perform a miraculous change in my life. I looked good, real good, on Sunday; but on the inside, I remained the same.

When no immediate change came I turned back to my weekend habits, drinking, smoking, chasing around with my friends on Friday and Saturday nights, and attending church on Sunday. This weekend habit wasn't as frequent or as enjoyable as it was before Eston's death, but I could not break myself. Church bored me. Many of the church members had the same problems I did and faked it on Sundays.

One outstanding lady, the pastor's wife at Second Baptist, Mrs. Zepphyr Clark, was for real. A sharp Christian lady, she loved the Lord, her husband, and the church. She reminded me of my grandmother, the kind of person I had to respect.

Many times she said to me, "If you change your life, give the Lord a chance, He will come into your life. You could really be a good Christian." I had added teaching Sunday

Image OF A Black Father

school on occasion to singing in the choir, and I thought *who are you to tell me what the Lord can do?* Despite this problem with her, I thought she was a wonderful lady. I even loved her. Mrs. Clark had been one of the first people I'd met when I came to Modesto. She'd invited Sherry, her mother and me over for tuna salad on toast and told us all about her city. We'd decided to move to Modesto because of her.

For two years I went on working weekdays, carousing Friday and Saturday nights and teaching Sunday school on Sunday. Then one day my mother-in-law and stepfather-in law and I had gone to a funeral. Sherry had gone to work for Gallo Winery by this time, so after the funeral all kinds of wine sat on our table, everybody having a glass, when Mrs. Clark came bouncing up the front walk. We had no time to put it all away, so I decided to meet her at the door.

Mrs. Clark said, "Do you mind if I come in?"

"Sure you can come in," I replied, embarrassed. Not knowing what else to do, I said, "Would you like a glass of wine?"

"No, I don't drink wine, but don't let me stop you," she answered. Then she continued, "One of the main reasons I came over is because Peter Johansen, a good friend of mine who goes to First Baptist Church, has invited some of us over to a Campus Crusade seminar. I went down and got the material for this Campus Crusade because I want you to go, Charlie, and represent our church."

Mrs. Clark had gained the respect of many white Christians. The one she'd mentioned in particular, Peter Johansen, served as mayor of Modesto for 12 years and was, as she'd said, a long-time member of First Baptist Church on the white side of Modesto. Skin color was not a problem for Pete. He came often to the West Side just to visit. He visited our churches and talked of ways to meet needs on the poor side of the tracks. He wasn't afraid to come alone, and no one stole his hubcaps.

Nevertheless, I asked, "Why me?"

"He wanted as many young people to come as possible. But I – I wanted *you* to go. I want you to go if nobody else goes."

I spread my feet apart, preparing to state my case strongly. Mrs. Clark made a formidable opponent. "I'm sorry, Mrs. Clark. I don't want to go. It's a big white church, and there's nothing over there but white people. I know there aren't going to be any black people over there, and I don't want to go. There'll be wall-to-wall white people, and I don't want to go. I just don't want to be around those white people."

With a polite smile, Mrs. Clark placed the seminar material on our coffee table. "I'm hoping you go and represent our young people," she said. "I bought the material, and it only cost $7. If you don't want to go, just throw it in the trash."

I knew what being poor meant. Mrs. Clark spending $7 on me wasn't something to ignore. She must have had a good reason to spend her $7 on me. I said, "All right, I'll think about it."

Monday morning, I got up and went to work at United Parcel Service. In the evening when I got home, the thing still lay on the coffee table. I thought, *well, why not*. I took a shower and then drove over to First Baptist, reluctantly, but I went. On the way, I told myself, *I'm just going to go over there and listen, but I'm not going to have any fun. Then I can go back and tell Ms. Clark that I did go.*

I liked the blue color the doors of First Baptist had been painted. They made a spot of cheerfulness in the white concrete face of the church. Inside, the carpet and pews were tinted the colors of the stained glass windows where the sun shone through. A few people were already seated on the cushioned pews. Folks on the white side of town had the money to make their places of worship comfortable and beautiful.

Most of the white folks stood in groups, talking and gesturing. By that time in my life there had been many times and places where mine was the only black face in the crowd. I felt lonely and out of place as I walked up to one of those groups.

Though I tried to smile and look comfortable so no one would see my fear, my lips got dry and my tongue got thick. I spoke carefully, trying to pronounce words correctly – "Hello, my name is Charlie."

Someone would say, "Hi, Kelly, glad to meet ya'." Usually, it would be women who greeted me first. They seemed to be more aware of my aloneness. I didn't want the white men to think I was being overfriendly to their women, so I would quickly divert my attention in any other direction. Thinking to myself, "I look like a fly in a glass of buttermilk," I decided I'd had this feeling so often, one more time wouldn't make any difference. So I found a soft seat on one of those cushioned pews.

That first evening Henry Schmidt was the man in charge of the Campus Crusade campaign. He was telling people what to do with the materials. He preached from I Peter 5 where in Verse 7 it says, "Cast all your anxiety on Him because He cares for you. ... your enemy, the devil, prowls around like a roaring lion ..."

I thought, *Wow, I need to cast all my cares on somebody, because things aren't working so far.*

Henry then said, "We're going to divide into groups of ten, go into separate rooms, and share with you the Four Spiritual Laws." The Four Spiritual Laws was a gospel tract put together by Bill Bright, the leader of Campus Crusade for Christ, for the purpose of sharing God's truth with college students.

My group went into a room called the Fireside Room because there was a fireplace in there. I heard that Law One said God loves you and has a wonderful plan for your life. Law Two said that man is sinful and separated from God. Law Three was the good news that Jesus Christ is God's only provision for man's sin. I had heard these things at church, but Law Four was my problem. It required that each person individually, receive Jesus Christ as Savior and Lord.

After discussing the Four Spiritual Laws, and realizing I'd never asked Jesus to come into my own heart to guide my life, I prayed, right there in the Fireside Room, to receive Christ as my Lord and Savior.

The groups returned to the auditorium, and for the first time in my life, I felt part of the worship that took place there. Henry Schmidt used the New International Version of the Holy Bible, and continued to focus on I Peter 5:7. The verse again caught my attention, "Cast all your anxiety on Him because He cares for you." I was a different man and knew that the Lord was speaking directly to me. I answered by whispering, "Lord, if You are really in my life, give me the power to stop drinking, smoking and chasing around." I had a pack of Winston cigarettes in my pocket. Right after I came out of the sanctuary, I took them out and laid them on the steps of the church.

I drove home after the seminar ended, talking to myself the whole way, because even as I drove I began reaching for a cigarette. *If the Lord is really in my life, He's going to have to give me the power to quit smoking, drinking and chasing women. He's going to have to show me how to make a good husband for my wife and father for my children because I can't do it by myself.*

The Lord was faithful. From that night, September 28, 1970, the sharecropper's son never smoked, drank or chased women again. I went home and became a husband to Sherry and a father to my children. I began reading the Gospel of John. I read through it five or six times before I realized that God had really saved me.

In order to get the chasing out of my system, I confessed to Sherry all I'd done. God was removing falsehood from my life, giving me the strange new desire to tell the truth.

Neither Sherry, nor God, talked to me for two weeks. To me, it seemed like two years.

Finally, after a long talk with her grandfather, Ward Ligons, who had cancer and lived with us, Sherry told me she still loved me. The two of us dropped out of our social clubs. I stopped attending Masonic Lodge meetings – and most of our friends dropped us.

When I realized God had truly saved me, I wanted to tell other people about my experiences. I went and bought a bunch of Four Spiritual Law booklets because I was going to do it on my own. However, I got an invitation from Campus Crusade to come to Arrowhead Springs, California, where their headquarters were. I figured they sent one to everyone they had the names of. I went down to Arrowhead Springs for a week to go to training on how to share the Four Spiritual Laws booklet. It felt wonderful getting to know God and His people amongst those pine trees. It felt even better sharing the little booklet with vacationers around Lake Arrowhead.

Back in Modesto I started to share the booklet with everyone I knew. Everybody started saying, "You should be a preacher."

I was thinking, I should go back to school, use the three other years of education Uncle Sam has given me to go to college, especially to learn how to read and understand the Bible better. Then I could tell people about the Lord, not be a preacher, just tell people about the Lord, especially my family.

I became a night student at Modesto Junior College (MJC), taking classes in speech, communication and reading comprehension. I went back over to Second Baptist, began singing in the choir and started a group of men who sang gospel songs. We called ourselves the Brotherhood Chorus.

However, I worried that my own brothers and sisters would never believe I had become a Christian. After all, I'd always been the life of the party. When our family came together, I was always the one telling the silly jokes and secretly mixing wine and vodka in the punch when Daddy wasn't looking. I didn't think they would believe I had changed. I wondered if they did believe me, whether they would still like me.

Then one day Mom called to let me know Grandmother Lucinda had become very ill. She had been taken to a hospital in Los Banos about 45 minutes from my house. I took a pastor with me and went to see her. She said in a weak voice, "I been waitin' a long time to go home. Please don't pray for healing. I am ready to go." The very next day, she saw Jesus with her own eyes.

At the memorial service, I said to my family, "I am going to become a preacher of the Gospel of Jesus Christ." They had no record of any preachers ever in our family line. The only example I had was that of a sharecropper. When I announced I was going to preach, no one knew how to respond. There was no excitement, backslapping, or rah-rah support. On the other hand, there were no discouraging words either, just a few stares of disbelief and an attitude of "wait and see." Except for Dad, who said, "Atta boy. That will be great." At that time, Mom and Dad were members of the Mt. Moriah Baptist Church in Dos Palos. After Lucinda's passing, their attendance became more regular.

Maybe because we had a large family, or maybe because as people get older more people they love pass away, the coming weeks and months held more tragedy. My brother, John's, birthday fell on April 11, which was Easter Sunday in 1971. Mom and Dad had gone to spend the weekend with John and his wife, Del, in Oakland. John had served in the

U.S. Army for eight years, doing a tour of duty on the front lines in Korea. Afterward, he suffered from post-traumatic stress syndrome.

If they hadn't been with John for Easter, Mom and Dad would probably have come to Modesto, where Willie and I lived, along with my sister, Wilma, who lived with her four boys in an apartment nearby. Saturday evening, the day before Easter, I went over to Wilma's place to invite her to church, and afterward to dinner at my house. She was separated from her husband and dating a man who had marriage problems of his own, so I thought she'd like to be with family for Easter. I found her apartment a mess.

The dishes weren't washed, the beds unmade, floor not swept, and the two smallest boys not dressed. Wilma's eyes were red, as though she'd been crying all day. I loved her. I tried to cheer her up. I'd talked to her about Jesus before and she'd even come to church. She'd sung in the choir a couple of times. Today, I wasn't even sure what to say. I didn't realize I shouldn't have left her alone in that condition, but I did.

Early Easter Sunday morning, just two weeks after the passing of our grandmother, Wilma killed herself. No one was sure whether it was purposeful, or a freak accident. The report said that her car had veered off the freeway overpass, landing upside down on the street below. This happened in Ceres at the Whitmore overpass, just five miles away, and only one exit from where Eston died. Wilma was only 24. She left four sons, Richard, 9; Derrall, 5; Terance, 3; and Eric, one and a half.

Dad had turned 74 that year. He and Mom had three children in their home: Edward Ray and Kathy, their two youngest children; and their oldest grandson, Kenneth. They insisted on caring for Wilma's three older boys. Sherry and I agreed to raise Eric with our three children. The father of the first three boys had moved to Boston and had no means to care for them. Eric's biological father's marriage problems kept him out of Eric's life.

Wilma's death struck the final blow to Dad. He lost his desire to work farms. He was in perfect health, but for the first time he felt he was getting too old to be a sharecropper. He told me, "My mind is tired of planting a crop year after year and watching the landowner rejoice over my profits. The truth is my children are my blessings from the Lord, and I want to spend the rest of my time being close to my children and grandchildren." I knew that Jab's family was the only joy he had in life. We were the fruit of his labor. The pain of watching us go, one by one, not knowing the destiny of our souls, was getting to be too much for him.

The six children now living in Dad's home saw him from a different perspective than his older children did. They saw a kind and gentle little man, waiting patiently for his monthly Social Security insurance check. They never knew or understood the bitter struggle that had brought him to this point in life. They never learned to appreciate and respect him, the sharecropper, for the toil and sacrifice he made for them and the rest of the family.

Sleep was the only freedom Jab knew. He had worked so hard and long he never had any free time to himself. Yet he never harbored anger or bitterness. Jab was the living example of a Bible passage in Exodus, Chapter 15:22-26:

"Then Moses led Israel from the Red Sea and they went into the desert of Shur. For three days, they traveled in the desert without finding water. When they came to Morah, they could not drink its water because it was bitter. (That is why the place is called Morah.) so the people grumbled against Moses, saying, "What are we to drink?"

Then Moses cried out to the lord and the Lord showed him a piece of wood. He threw it into the water and the water became sweet.

There the Lord made a decree and a law for them. He said, "If you listen carefully to the voice of the Lord, your God and do what is right in His eyes, if you pay attention to His commands and keep all His decrees, I will not bring on you any of the diseases I brought on the Egyptians, for I am the Lord Who heals you."

Then they came to Elim where there were twelve springs of water and seventy palm trees, and they camped there near the water."

Dad had been emptied of the world's natural spirit, the craving of sinful man, the lust of the eyes, and the boasting of what he has and does. Racial discrimination and civil oppression had left him inwardly bitter toward the established system, a spirit that God only could change. Maybe it was through the death of three of his children, happening at three-year intervals, that God showed him a piece of wood – the cross of Christ.

In the time when Dad stopped working, he also stopped smoking, and started trusting God for his daily bread. He bought a new Bible, a fishing license, and a rod and reel. With only his third grade education, he was able to read and comprehend God's word. He became a deacon in his church.

He listened carefully to God's word, and did what was right in His eyes by loving God and people, giving his time and what little money he had. He even raised fruit and vegetables in his backyard, both for our family and to share with the people around him. The one deadly disease that plagued Egypt and is so prevalent in our world today is hate, the hardening of the heart. God did not allow this disease to come upon Jab. He gave him a love and respect for all mankind.

Willie and I moved Mom and Dad and the rest of family to Modesto in 1972. Sherry and I had moved to a house on Shirley Court. After remodeling the garage into a den,

Jab and Cordie moved into our old house. They joined the Second Baptist Church where Dad was appointed to the board of deacons and Mom joined the choir. For the first time since the Cranes left Arkansas, we were worshipping God together in the same camp. I wished my grandmother could have seen it.

Chapter Nine

Black Church/White Church

The Brotherhood Chorus at Second Baptist was starting to sound like a professional group. Popular, we received invitations from various religious groups in the area to perform in services and on special occasions. Chester Smith, the owner of local television Channel 19, gave our gospel group 30 minutes a week of free time. J.C. Penney provided uniforms for all the men in the group. I thought we looked better than we sounded.

However, a problem arose. The TV show aired every Sunday from 7-7:30 p.m. Pastor Howard Clark said it disrupted his Second Baptist evening service, which also began at 7 p.m. He complained that most of the congregation missed the evening service to watch what were now called the Spiritulaires on TV.

The group tried to compromise with Pastor Clark, by suggesting he come and preach for 15 minutes, and then we'd sing for 15 minutes, but he complained the louder. He would not join us in an evening service on TV, nor would he change the schedule of the evening service. Pastor Clark pointed his finger at me for starting all this conflict. After several weeks of bickering, the Spiritulaires gave up on T.V. to keep peace with our pastor. By this time, my relationship with Pastor Clark was severely damaged. Pastor Clark started to keep me at a distance and diminished my relationship with the singing group.

Pastor Clark, though a small man in stature, behaved aggressively. He involved himself in civil rights, black politics and community activities. He helped a lot of people, but not without obligation. He needed authority over everyone he had shown favor to.

The final break in our relationship came when the Spiritulaires received an invitation to present a musical program for Mt. Moriah Baptist Church in Dos Palos. About six weeks in advance, the singing group politely asked Rev. Clark permission to honor this invitation. He granted permission, and the event and its date were written on the church calendar.

However, the Second Baptist choir members saw the date on the calendar and decided to join the Spiritulaires on their trip to Dos Palos to support them and help make the event a success. When Pastor Clark heard the choir planned to go with the Spiritulaires, he thought the singing group was interfering with the evening service again. Immediately he made plans designed to stop the choir from going to Dos Palos.

One week prior to the calendar event for Mt. Moriah Baptist, Pastor Clark announced in the Sunday morning service that the entire church body were invited to guest host a celebration for his best friend's pastoral anniversary, which was going to be held in Stockton on the same date and at the same time as the Dos Palos program.

I went to him and said, "Reverend Clark, you said it was all right for us to go to Dos Palos."

The reverend replied, "Yeah, well that was before I got the call from the brother in Stockton. You'll have to change your plans. I've already chartered a bus. We're all riding over on the same bus." In his excitement, Pastor Clark chartered a bus to transport the entire congregation, including the singing groups.

I felt at this point any effort to compromise with my pastor would be futile. I replied, "You shouldn't have done that, because we're already committed to these people to go down to Dos Palos. They're counting on us.

They've invited all kinds of people to come hear us and donate to the building of the church. If we don't go, they can't have their service."

"I'm sorry, but I want everybody to go to Stockton."

I shook my head, and said, "Well, I'll go back and tell the guys."

I did, and they said they wanted to go to Dos Palos, and so did the choir. Without bickering, the Spiritulaires went to Dos Palos, along with the choir.

Reverend Clark had no one on his bus. He was seeing-red angry.

The following week a few women from the choir went to the church to perform their usual chores, only to discover that their keys didn't work. Pastor Clark had changed all the locks. When they called him, they were told to reaffirm their commitment to the church.

On Sunday morning, when the congregation arrived for the service, Reverend Clark had called the sheriffs, who stood waiting for them. When the congregation questioned his authority, he said, "I own Second Baptist Church. All the property of the church is in my name, and my name only. I can and I will have you escorted from my property." After finishing an argument with the deacons, the pastor told me, "Thanks for the service you have rendered."

Astonished, I asked, "*Have* rendered?"

"Yes, *have* rendered. You go in there and sit with the congregation."

I replied, "You're quite welcome," gathered Sherry and our kids, and left Second Baptist. I didn't believe there should be any landowners in the family of God. Since Pastor Clark clearly did, it was time for me to go. I hadn't wanted to be a sharecropper on the farms, and no one but God was going to make me one in the church.

My parents, brothers and sisters stayed at Second Baptist. Dad would know how to love this man. This man was a landowner. Being a sharecropper, Jab knew, from experience, how to love him. At least, I knew he would try.

As I drove away, an outcast, I began to think. Because of the powerful influence Pastor Clark had among the local churches, I felt my small reputation as a minister was over. No other West Side pastor who knew Pastor Clark would take a chance on accepting me. It occurred to me that it was possible God wanted me to move, and was using Pastor Clark to get it done. At any rate, I needed a place of refuge, a place to hide and wait on the Lord. However, though being an outcast was very difficult to accept, returning to my old lifestyle never entered my mind.

As I considered what to do, First Baptist Church loomed in my mind, and I drove in that direction. It would be the perfect place. The black people would not look for me there, and the white people would not want to be involved. Pretty much like David among the Philistines, I could sit in the pews and foam at the mouth. Maybe they would say, "This man is crazy and is not a threat to us."

It was at First Baptist Church that I had met Jesus. Now I believed this urge to return was my Lord telling me He had pushed me this way, was going with me and waiting for me there.

That Sunday morning service at First Baptist was packed out – wall to wall people, all white, well-dressed, upper middle class professional people, business people, educators, politicians, etc. This was no place for a sharecropper's son. They would have no need for me to say or do anything here. Sherry and I sat on the first level of pews near the back and tried to look inconspicuous, when all along we felt as if we were the elephant in the room.

The sermon was more than I expected. The pastor, Bill Yaeger, spoke in his natural voice. He didn't yell or scream, nor did he whoop, thump his Bible, or pound the pulpit. In a normal but sincere tone his message pulled the focus of the entire congregation to the cross of Christ where Jesus went out of His way to allow us to have a relationship with God and with one another.

By the end of his sermon, I was thoroughly convinced that God had brought me here to build relationships with a group of people I didn't even like.

The next Sunday, Pastor Yaeger gave an invitation for anyone wishing to receive Christ as Lord and Savior to come forward. I went forward to ask, "How do I get involved as a servant of the Lord?" A prayer room counselor met with me to gather necessary information to assist me in pursuing my spiritual goals.

My family had only been at First Baptist a short time when Pastor Clark heard we were attending there. He called Pastor Yaeger and told him all about my "troublemaking." Pastor Yaeger was intrigued, and had his secretary, Maxine Lewis, call me to come in for an appointment.

When I walked into Pastor Yaeger's office, Pastor shook my hand and offered me a seat. Then he said, "I got a call from Pastor Clark over on the West Side. He told me a whole lot of stuff about you, so I just had to meet you."

He began relating some of the things Pastor Clark had said, and then he leveled his ice-blue eyes at me, and said, "Is any of that stuff true?"

I answered, "Well, from his point of view it is."

Pastor Yaeger laughed, and said, "Then I'm glad you left. If you really want to be a preacher, and a leader in a church, I can help you do that."

In shock, I answered eloquently. "OK."

Pastor Yaeger explained to me his role as senior pastor of First Baptist Church. He told me he had developed a program to train and send out young people to do the same work he did, but in other parts of the world. "How much schooling do you have?" Pastor asked.

"I've finished the twelfth grade, but right now I'm going to MJC taking night classes, because I work during the day. I'm trying to learn how to read and understand better."

Pastor said, "Well, don't stop going to school then. We're developing an extension branch of Simpson College.

If you want to go that route, the church could help finance your education and your practical training would be done at First Baptist."

I was floored that a white man who cared about a black man would help me succeed.

Chapter Ten

I Cain't Go to School!

I was 36 in 1972. Sherry and I had four children and a nephew, Eric, living with us. Our youngest daughter, Shdrai, was only nine months old. "Pastor, I am not able to give up my day job," I said, hoping against hope that something could be worked out. I had thought formal education in the ministry merely a dream.

Pastor Yaeger responded, "God gives gifts to men and with those gifts, the responsibility to develop them. You'll work it out."

Sherry and I began attending a Sunday school class for new members. Our kids were in classes appropriate to their ages. We all found new friends and personal relationships. We began to feel comfortable in our large white, and now black, church. After six weeks of new members' classes, Sherry and I joined "King's couples," a Sunday Bible study for married couples in our age group.

We were having fun at church and at home. Life was great, but I still wanted to meet Pastor Yaeger's challenge of developing God's gift.

Yet my family had to come first. Dad had taught me that the security and well being of the family were my primary goal. UPS only offered one nighttime position. I approached the manager with a request to work that night job, and the two of us agreed. I took a job no employee was better suited for – washing trucks. As a teamster's union member, I received no cut in pay.

Pastor Walter C. (Bud) La Core, who Pastor Yaeger had asked to move into full-time ministry from his vocation as owner of a tire company, now served as First Baptist's Minister of Development. He showed me, and hundreds of others over the years, how to manage our finances. He said, "Tithe on 100% of your income."

Someone in the crowd asked, "Before or after taxes?"

Pastor La Core, whom most people called Uncle Bud, replied, "What do you want to be blessed on, the gross or the net?"

He went on to say, "Put away at least 10% of what you make for emergencies and 10% for savings. Live on the other 70%."

I began to follow Uncle Bud's advice, and it worked.

As soon as I had a night job, I enrolled in a full load of classes at MJC and in the intern program at First Baptist.

The student affairs clerk asked, "Charlie, why aren't you using your veteran's benefits?"

"Up until now, I've been attending part time," I answered. I thought about the bills I owed that resulted from my family trying to keep up with the Joneses. I filled out the paperwork for veteran's benefits, and with the $400 I got each month, I paid our debts.

In 1974, the same year the Simpson College extension opened at First Baptist Church, I graduated from MJC. Following Pastor Yaeger's wise counsel, I enrolled in Simpson College, worked full-time at night and slept when I could catch a few hours. Pastor Yaeger, true to his word, never let any of the interns see a bill for their studies at Simpson.

Not only that, but he saw that the single ones had spending money and to the married guys he gave a job if they needed one. I was different. I had a job, so Pastor Yaeger only paid for my schooling. I marched across the stage first at the initial graduating ceremony of Simpson College Modesto in June 1976.

In celebration of our nation's bicentennial birthday, the church presented a musical production, **Freeman**, written and directed by Lin Sexton, Pastor Yaeger's daughter. The play chronicled the history of the United States through four performances with almost 10,000 people in attendance. I felt free enough to participate in this great event at my primarily white church. I played the role of a slave, standing bare-chested in chains on the stage before all those white folks.

Freeman, played by Ray Newman, came to me and said, "How can you say you're free?"

I responded, "These chains don't bind my heart. My spirit has been set free." I sang, "This world is not my home, I'm just a passin' through. If Heaven's not my home, then Lord what would I do? The angels beckon me to Heaven's open door, and I ain't gonna' live in this world anymore, Oh Lord, you know I have no friend like you." As I sang, I knew God had removed all racial bitterness from my life and replaced it with love, a kingdom love for God and for all of God's people.

During that summer, tragedy struck our family again. Relatives were visiting my sister in her Ceres apartment. While the women talked inside, the children played in the backyard. A cyclone fence separated the kids from an irrigation canal running at full capacity. The kids discovered an opening in the fence just large enough for them to crawl through. The Cranes lost three-year-old Bird and two-year-old Cocoa to that canal. Cocoa was Jab's granddaughter by his youngest daughter, Kathy. Bird was Jab's great grandson by his oldest daughter of Cordie's, Dot.

This new loss affected Dad, now 79, who though he functioned as strongly as ever, both physically and mentally, began to noticeably rely on me. He began pushing my opinions to the front and fostering my ideas. Dad was leading the family to build their confidence in me. I felt honored because my father saw me as someone serious enough and capable enough, probably because of my graduation from college and intention to go into ministry, to be the family leader. However, Jab's character hadn't come from a book, and I hoped I had watched my father carefully enough to fill his shoes.

While I studied for the ministry Pastor Yaeger gave me an open door to his office, as he did all the interns. However, we had to get past his secretary, Maxine Lewis, whom he and everyone else called Max. This was not an easy task, as Max had a keen understanding of the breakneck schedule Pastor Yaeger kept. One day I asked Pastor Yaeger how to get past Max.

Pastor replied, "You know there are back stairs to my office. Come that way.

I imagine you're used to that." Only Pastor could have made that joke and heard me laugh. I never actually tried the back stairs, though. It was too presumptuous, and besides, it wasn't good to get on the bad side of Max.

The interns referred to Pastor Yaeger's office as the Bear's Den. Shortly after I graduated from Simpson, Max permitted entrance to the Bear's Den where the Bear stood waiting. He clapped me on the back and gave me a hug. I began, "My family and I are so grateful for all the love and kindness you and the church have shown us, especially for my schooling."

Image OF A Black Father

Pastor Yaeger stopped me in mid-thought, saying, "Now, you need your work permit."

"Work permit?"

"Yes, work permit. A Bachelor of Arts degree is good. It shows you went to school, but an M.A. says that you are ready to work and to show others how to do it."

He proceeded to tell me about an arrangement he had worked out for his interns to attend the Mennonite Brethren Biblical Seminary in Fresno, about 100 miles south of Modesto, also paid for by the church.

Not long after, at age 40, with a full-time job to support my wife and four children, I enrolled at the Mennonite Brethren Biblical Seminary to get my work permit. I wanted to be a sharecropper for the Master, like the men I honored, Jab and Pastor Yaeger.

The interns spent one day per week on the Fresno campus and two days per week on the First Baptist campus under the tutelage of Dr. Eddie Sivertsen. Six of us got together and carpooled to Fresno. My schedule made it imperative that we drive pretty fast to get back to Modesto so I could arrive at my night job on time. However, one intern, a huge man from Oklahoma named Jim Talley insisted on driving the speed limit. He said, "If you're a Christian, you're supposed to be obedient to the laws of the land." On the days it was Jim's turn to drive, I would sweat all the way back to Modesto.

We interns worked at the church in our major fields of interest. Preaching interns were sent to Modesto Union Gospel Mission, a homeless shelter; youth camps and other churches. Some were granted the privilege to speak at First Baptist. I was one of those. It happened late in the summer of 1976. Pastor asked me to preach the two evening services. When he saw the frightened look on my face, he added these encouraging words, "The people here love you. You'll do well."

Pastor had supplied all the confidence I needed. I had become a fully accepted member of this local family in the body of Jesus Christ, and not as the black sheep of the family, either. The color of my skin, my brown eyes and wooly hair would no longer be a problem for me. The fact that I spoke with a southern drawl and had never learned the proper use of grammar did not matter. My lips would get dry and tongue thick; but that, too, would be OK because God had appointed me to speak to his own family. They all loved me, and I would do well.

Pastor Yaeger had been teaching the interns' homiletics (how to preach a sermon) class. As I prepared to speak, many of the pulpit manners Pastor had taught us ran through my head. *Don't ever wear a lime green suit; don't jingle your change; don't wear a blood red tie to a funeral; don't ever use the word genuwine, if you don't know how to pronounce genuine, just avoid it; don't be afraid to call a spade a spade.* Those were some of the Yaegerisms I remembered about preaching. As my Sunday approached, many others floated through my head. *You put a big frog in a small pond, and he croaks. Everybody stops and listens. You move that same frog to a big pond and he croaks, and the others say, "Did you hear something?* Or *Paint a door blue, then you'll find out who is there to worship God and who is there just for the looks.* Or *First Baptist stays downtown. Let the rest of them move to the outskirts, away from the homeless, the poor. We're serving those downtown. Let the rest come here.*

On that evening I spoke from John 8:31-32. I chose the title, "The Truth Will Set You Free."

Through Pastor Yaeger, God had made it known to me that His truth had set me free – free from depression caused by my anger toward oppression and ill treatment at the hands of evil men; free from the bitterness of slavery and civil injustice done to people in the past that still causes racial prejudice and hatred to linger in the hearts of many today. I was free from those inward emotions that rob a man of the joy of being a man. When I finished the sermon, Pastor said, "You did great. You'll make a good preacher."

Pastor Yaeger was a sharecropper like Jab. He reared up and trained children to work the Master's fields. The Owner of the fields had supplied him with the tools to do the labor. At the end of the day, he too, would share in the harvest. Like Jab, Pastor Yaeger became my father, in ministry rather than physically, and I knew my only obligation to Pastor lay in the continuing debt of love.

I came to believe that the Good Samaritan was my favorite story in all the Holy Bible because it told how Jesus healed us with His love and commanded us to heal our relationships in the same manner.

... A man was going down from Jerusalem to Jericho, when he fell into the hands of robbers. They stripped him of his clothes, beat him and went away, leaving him half dead. A priest happened to be going down the same road, and when he saw the man, he passed by on the other side. So too, a Levite, when he came to the place and saw him, passed by on the other side. But a Samaritan, as he traveled, came where the man was; and when he saw him, he took pity on him. He went to him and bandaged his wounds, pouring on oil and wine. Then, he put the man on his own donkey, took him to an inn and took care of him. The next day he took out two silver coins and gave them to the innkeeper. 'Look after him,' he said, 'and when I return, I will reimburse you for any extra expense you may have.' (Luke 10:30-35, NIV)

I saw myself as the victim in this story – one who had sinned and fallen short of the glory of God; one robbed of love, joy and peace of mind. Stripped of any righteousness that could hide my guilt in the presence of God, my sin was shamefully exposed. Fear had beaten me, left me spiritually dead and physically helpless.

The priest came by, but had no salvation with him. His religion could not save me. Likewise, the Levite, with all his theological training, when he saw my condition, had to pass me by. His education was good, but powerless to heal a guilty conscience or resurrect a dead spirit.

I saw the Lord Jesus Christ portrayed by the Samaritan in this parable. By nature, the Samaritan was half Jew and half Gentile. God broke the dividing wall that separated God's people from the pagan world and the two met in the one body of the Samaritan. By the Holy Spirit, Jesus was born God and man. The Spirit of God and the spirit of man met in the one body of Jesus, making Him the only mediator between man and God.

When He saw my condition, He took pity on me. He came to me and covered my guilt and shame. Pouring on the oil of peace and the wine of joy, He restored my soul. He took all my anxiety upon Himself because He cared for me. Jesus took me into His Church and paid the Holy Spirit, the keeper of His Church, to look after me. Jesus said, "When I return, I will reimburse you for any grief he may have caused you."

That fall of 1978 our family lost another member. Someone killed my brother, John, in a poolroom brawl. John was a Korean War veteran. He had served in front line combat in 1952 and 1953. After Korea he wanted to remain in the Armed Forces, but he suffered from post-traumatic stress syndrome and alcohol dependency. He often engaged in barroom brawls and went A.W.O.L. Instead of continuing to serve his country, he received an honorable discharge with medical disability in 1958. John came home at age 26, legally blind and diagnosed with macular degeneration. With these problems and only an eighth grade education, John had no hope of a normal life. He had given his best years for his country. His death was not unexpected, the news not shocking, though painful and sad.

The police called Charlie to the scene about 4 a.m. on Sunday to make identification. No traffic moved on the streets; the pool hall lay vacated and cold. Charlie saw no sign of a struggle – no broken glass or furniture. Only one police officer waited, with Art Baker, who interned with me at First Baptist Church and moonlighted as a mortician. Art expressed his sympathy and said he needed a signed statement of identification. John's body lay uncovered in the middle of the floor in a fetal position with a single gunshot to his head from a small caliber gun. I thought, "God, it was clean, not a messy scene."

I don't know where or when we lost John, whether in Korea in 1953 or at the pool hall in 1978; but I knew the family loved him and prayed often for him. Now God would determine his destination. We laid John to rest with full military honors. Jab showed no outward emotion except for a sad countenance and his wrinkled nose, but I felt his pain. I wanted to reach out to Jab.

I wanted to lay aside my busy schedule and spend time with my dad, Mom and the rest of my family. I tried to find extra time for them when I could, but the pace of everyone's life made the time precious little.

The interns finished the graduate work at the seminary in June of 1979. I thought of this graduation as "we" rather than "I" because Sherry's name should be included, in the front. She had done the hard work of caring for me and five children. She had made my graduation possible. Sherry and Charlie Crane now had a work permit, an M.A. in Christian Education.

Pastor Yaeger offered me a position with his staff at First Baptist and wanted me to call him by his first name, "Bill."

I declined both offers and with good reason. Regarding the first, I had been away from my family's church for seven years.

Now the time had come to return.

As for the second, Pastor Yaeger had impacted my life in such a way that I would always honor and respect him as "Pastor," never Bill. With Pastor's blessing, I returned to the West Side of the tracks.

Chapter 11

Back to the Other Side of the Tracks

Sherry, our five kids and I began our return to the West Side when we joined Bethany Baptist, one of the five churches there. Our attendance increased its membership by 25 percent since the congregation was small. I chose this new church because I admired the pastor, Rev. Kenoli, a well-built man with large biceps and salt and pepper hair. I thought Rev. Kenoli and his congregation might have an open door for new ideas. Bethany's pastor held a second job at Sharp Army Depot because the congregation wasn't large enough to support his family, so I hoped their minister would also be open to having help.

Rev. Kenoli welcomed me into his study one day soon after we began attending Bethany, and we shared coffee while we talked.

I said, "Pastor, I don't know what you may have heard about me, but I have no intention of coming back to the West

Side to take over. I want to help you teach and preach. I'm a Tonto, not a Lone Ranger."

Rev. Kenoli pulled at his mustache and asked, "What do you think the priorities of the church should be, Charlie?"

Without hesitation, I answered, "Evangelism and discipleship."

"All right, then," Rev. Kenoli said. "Let's work together."

Sherry and I began teaching evangelism and tithing right after this meeting.

After a few weeks of serving at Bethany, several black pastors invited me to meet with them. During the meeting they asked if I would run for a chair on the Modesto City Council in the upcoming election. They claimed they picked me because I had been on the powerful side of town and knew lots of people, like Peter Johansen, who served in government. I declined, stating my desire to preach and teach Jesus as Lord.

None of them had a membership large enough to support a full-time pastor. To them, I represented another frog in a pond already too full of frogs. I thought they wanted me on the city council to get me out of their preaching competition. Once I declined to run, the pastors brushed me aside and stopped speaking to me. I again was free to minister in whatever way the Lord led.

There was much talk on the West Side about opening the doors of black churches to include other races and ethnic groups. "Whosoever will, let him come," is a cry heard in all Christian churches, but the struggle among the races is, "Who's in control?" A lot of Hispanic people as well as the boat people from Vietnam were beginning to settle on the West Side. However, no black people had gone out of their way to draw these people into the churches.

I felt pastors should strive to be sharecroppers for the Lord, but instead competed with each other for ownership. Because of this, the church had a difficult time coming together in any town. Each pastor asked, "Who's in control?" with the thought that he should be.

As long as they did this, the work of the Lord struggled to go forward, except on a basis limited to the local congregation. I knew a sharecropper doesn't own anything. He shares everything – that is his challenge and his pledge, yet many pastors didn't see their role as sharecroppers. At any rate, I told them my plan was just to work with Rev. Kenoli at Bethany to reach all the people they could, black, brown, yellow or white, which I did, for about a year. The church began to grow, filling with all ages and races.

The best invitation I received after returning to the West Side came from a portion of the old Second Baptist Church congregation from 1979. They still had disputes with Rev. Clark and had begun meeting in the home of Deacon Parker, who was part of the group. The six deacons in this group included Dad. My dad and mom were my reason for accepting their invitation to meet with them.

First, I intended to convince them to return to their church. If that failed, I hoped they'd choose to join Bethany Baptist or any other existing West Side church. I felt there didn't need to be another Baptist Church on the West Side.

They met one evening at Deacon Parker's home. His wife, a tall lady whose face always clearly indicated her mood, and Mom were good friends. They sang in the choir together. Mrs. Parker was the strong, outspoken one in the family. She felt free to express her opinion in her own home, and did. Both my plans were totally rejected by the deacon group. Mrs. Parker, hands on hips, said, "Hey, no, we won't go back to Second Baptist, and we don't want to join Rev. Kenoli's congregation. We need our own church!"

Since Plans A and B didn't work, I gave in. The timing was perfect for me to have time to work with the group to organize a new church.

Our youngest, Shdari, was in school full time. Sherry had taken a day job with Bronco Winery; and I had accepted a management position with U.P.S. working a graveyard shift, which afforded me time to work with this group.

I wouldn't have considered such a thing had not Dad been part of it. He explained to me, "We don't want to bother with Rev. Clark anymore. We just want to worship on our own, and not cause trouble for anyone else." I could see that Rev. Clark would make things difficult for this group of people no matter where they went. I wanted to help them persevere.

The group rented a storefront building for space large enough to house Sunday gatherings for worship and Bible study. We hired attorney, Paul Fulfer, a member of First Baptist Church, to help with the legal work, which he did without charge. Someone donated a piano, and a cabinet-maker in the group built a small podium. We held a name choosing, where everyone put in a possibility and we voted.

In May of 1980 the group became the congregation of the True Light Baptist Church, a name chosen by Deacon Jab. Dad chose from the Gospel of John, where it talks about the True Light coming into the world. Everyone liked it. However, the name was rejected by the Secretary of State because of its similarity to the name of another organization in the area. Therefore, the Modesto congregation became the Greater True Light Baptist Church.

When the landlord discovered that we had organized into a religious body, he wanted to raise the rent. We began disputing over our contract with him while looking for another rental that would meet their needs. We had no finances or credit. However, my job was finished; the group had everything they needed to be a church, except a pastor. They would have to choose for themselves.

I told the congregation, "Please, do not vote for me for senior pastor. I don't want to be a senior pastor, I want to help, to teach, but not to administer a whole church."

Knowing they were leaning toward calling me to be their pastor anyway, I said, "However, If you do include me in your vote, I won't accept unless the vote is 100%."

After all, one of the deacons had a son who was ministering in the Bay Area. He wanted to come to Modesto. I assumed his father would vote against me, and that would take care of the 100% vote.

Sherry and I took the kids on a two-week vacation to Ohio. On our return, a trio of deacons came to visit me. Dad was one of the three. Deacon Johnson, a six-foot husky man with a big smile, was their spokesman, and Dad didn't say a whole lot. I figured Dad didn't want me to think he was pressuring me to be the pastor if I didn't want to do it.

"Charlie, we have gone through a long, tedious process of nominating and voting you to be our senior pastor with a starting salary of $350 per month," Deacon Johnson said.

I knew that this long tedious process came from the fact that many of them were, or had been, Masons.

They had voted with black and white marbles. If a deacon were for me, he put a white marble in the box. If he were against, he put in a black marble.

I asked, "Were there any black marbles in the box?"

"Not a one," they replied.

Dad sat quietly, letting Deacon Johnson do the talking. I appreciated my father leaving the decision to me.

"Then I will be your pastor," I said.

If Dad thought there was room for another church, then I thought there was room.

Just before I agreed to be pastor of Greater True Light Baptist Church, the Paradise Christian Reformed Church had moved to the north side of Modesto and sold their West Side facility to another religious organization. The new owner of the West Side property did the necessary repairs and some cosmetic work. The outside of the building needed a paint job, and the inside had mahogany stained beams on the ceiling that made the church look dark.

The repairs included new flooring in the social hall, lighter paint, new fire extinguishers, a refrigerator and servicing the air conditioners. Despite all their repairs, for some unknown reason they placed the property for sale. Our congregation made an appointment for the whole group to see this property.

Everyone loved this church, but we couldn't afford the listed price. We joined hands in a circle, and several led prayer for God to purchase this facility for us anyway. Meanwhile, our landlord was planning to increase the monthly rate on his storefront property after one year. Two months passed. Then we heard the Paradise property would be auctioned to the highest bidder. The owner wanted what was owed on the property, $124,522. Our deacon board obtained the date, time and place of the sale.

Then we called Pastor Yaeger for help. Without hesitation, he brought the board members of the two churches together to decide what they could do and how to make it happen.

Pastor Yaeger sent real estate man, Allen Grant, to get an estimated value of the property. Grant answered that the property was worth $212,000, what the owners had originally asked. Then Pastor asked me, "What do you think it would take to get that church?"

I answered, "We could handle payments on up to $175,000."

Pastor then sent Don Bodes, the First Baptist business manager, who'd been a banker before he came to work at the church, to find a bank that would loan the new church the money. Don, a quiet man, and I went from bank to bank, but no one wanted to loan money to a church. Finally, we went to Modesto Banking Company, a local bank where First Baptist did their banking. They didn't want to loan the money either. So Don said, "Then make the loan to First Baptist Church."

"We wouldn't be interested in that either," the loan officer said.

Don got mad.

He jumped up, red-faced, slammed his brief case in the middle of the floor and exclaimed, "We do over a million dollars of business a year with your bank, and you don't want to loan us $175,000? That's OK. Just close our account, and I'll be down here to sign the papers." We took off.

In the car, he turned to me and said, "By the time we get to the office we'll have somebody from the bank calling us."

We drove back the three blocks to his office at the church. As soon as we walked in, his secretary said, "Modesto Banking Company called, and they want you to come back in to see them."

Don said, "Get them back on the phone first." Once they were on, he said, "I don't mind coming to the bank, but what am I coming for? Am I closing our accounts, or getting the loan?"

"You're coming to get the loan."

"Make the $175,000 in cashier's checks, $25,000 each."

Don and I went back an hour later, and the bank had the checks ready. It was a Friday, and the Greater True Light deacon board had to be at the auction at 7 a.m. Monday morning. We purchased the church with all its furniture for about one half of its estimated value, and $1 more than the opening bid.

The True Light family moved into its new home in March 1981 with the purchase loan agreement extended on a 20-year contract. I felt proud to be their pastor. I prayed

God would allow me to serve with them for the entire 20 years, so I could make sure they paid off the building and didn't have any outstanding loans that First Baptist church was responsible for.

The entire congregation of Greater True Light Baptist Church went to First Baptist for my ordination service. All the First Baptist ministerial staff laid hands on Sherry and I, prayed, and presented me a Certificate of Ordination, showing their approval and support for the ministry at Greater True Light. That love and support between all those white and black people left me amazed.

However, the ultimate test of Sherry and my faith was coming in late March of 1982. We had just gotten into bed one night when the phone rang. It was Cliff Sexton, a classmate and colleague from First Baptist Church. Cliff told me he was at Scenic General Hospital when the paramedics brought in a young man involved in a vehicle accident.

"He may be your son, Kurry," he said. "You and Sherry should come out here." Cliff spoke calmly with a steady voice when he said he would meet us in the lobby. I tried to be as calm and steady when I relayed the message to Sherry.

The ride to the hospital that night seemed an hour although we were only about two miles away. We prayed the whole distance, trying to prepare ourselves for the worst while hoping for the best.

Cliff was waiting as we entered the lobby. He said, "Let me pray with you; then I will take you to him."

My heart sank as Cliff prayed. I knew my son was seriously injured, and I felt so afraid, I though I might collapse.

I wanted to apologize to the Lord for being afraid, but I had no energy. My knees were weak, and I needed to sit down. I avoided eye contact with Sherry, because I was afraid I'd burst into tears. It was not time to cry yet. Cliff introduced us to a nurse who told us Kurry was in X-ray. Shortly after that, the doctor told us our son had massive injuries to his head, and chances of recovery were slim. For 14 hours Sherry and I sat in the waiting room.

Again and again the silent waiting was broken when one of them would say, "Lord, please, please Lord, heal our child, let us keep our boy, Father, please." Even in the silence, I prayed, and I knew Sherry did, too. We hoped, because God can do anything. Our daughters and Willie came and sat with us. Others came and went. Tuesday afternoon, March 29, 1982 Kurry was pronounced dead. God had chosen to take him to Heaven.

A young man driving under the influence of alcohol caused Kurry's death. He carried a valid driver's license and liability insurance; but he was legally drunk. He was so drunk he didn't know he had caused an accident until several hours later.

Kurry's girlfriend, Salena, was a passenger with him. Critically injured in the crash, she was taken to a different hospital. Because of her poor mental and physical condition, no one told her Kurry had died until several weeks after the funeral. Her family were members of True Light. The accident left no visible scars to her beauty, but her heart and mind were scarred forever. Both families agreed not to sue or attempt to destroy the life of the young man who foolishly caused them so much hurt and pain. No amount of money or time spent in jail could correct or justify the cost of the suffering after Kurry's death.

With all the times the Cranes had encountered death in our family, I felt I should have known how to handle these kinds of things, but when it was Kurry, my only son, I didn't.

This time a part of me died, a part that could never be replaced or healed. I started a confused monologue to God. "God what have I done to deserve this? Before when I acted crazy, You might have used it to get my attention, but now I've been a Christian for twelve years. Nine of these years I spent in school, preparing for the ministry. I'm a pastor now, being good – doing good things should count for something. Isn't there some kind of special treatment for pastors?"

God didn't answer. I could only drag myself through each day, doggedly putting one foot in front of the other.

Sherry and I couldn't talk to one another about how we felt. It hurt too painfully. Friends and relatives all around supported and comforted us, but we felt alone and lonely.

Dad came over to be with me frequently. He didn't say anything, nor did he look directly at me. He didn't hug or pat me on the back. Nor did either of us weep.

As in times past, I could see the hurt in Dad's face. The line creased his nose again. I remembered seeing that look before.

However, it was as if Dad knew his visible presence would be enough to renew my hope. Perhaps Jab hoped that remembering my father had faced this kind of pain and persevered, would help me come to grips with the pity I felt for myself. Eventually, I would realize the same Power that had brought my dad through his hours of grief four times would bring me through mine as well.

Our bedroom was in the front part of the house. Despite reality, I would hear Kurry's car pull to a stop in the street outside. Sometimes I got up and looked out, hoping to see my son coming up our walkway. Sometimes I listened from bed, waiting to hear the front door open. After a few minutes of waiting I would realize it was only a dream. My spirit was in the denial stage of grief. Kurry was gone, and there was no way to bring him back.

Sherry and I felt as though we had been robbed, raped, and cheated out of something that could never be replaced.

We had no son who would carry our name into the next generation. Our daughters had no brother to be uncle to their children. To avoid thinking of this or engaging in conversation that would recall these painful moments, I busied myself in my work at U.P.S. during the early morning hours and at True Light during the day. I kept busy at home in the evenings. Kurry's senseless death still gnawed at me, though.

Chapter Twelve

Coming Home

To everything there is a season. In my season of suffering, I came to realize that a dream I'd had for a long time might happen through the death of my son. The fulfillment of my dream could bring a measure of meaning to the pain in my life. I had begun to worry from the time I became a Christian about boys growing up with no direction or model. I'd had an honest, hardworking model in my dad, and I'd still chosen the wrong path at times. I couldn't imagine how a boy who had no father at hand could find his way into manhood in a strong, healthy, right way.

I'd seen many boys without fathers in their homes come to the age of twelve or thirteen, begin to feel the leadership inclinations that God puts in men, and want to exercise them. When no dad lived in the house, they felt the responsibility to be the dad.

Their mothers weren't about to allow their sons to do that, so the boys began to run away and get into trouble. With no dads to guide and protect them, they argued and got into fights with other children. They couldn't have the "my daddy is bigger than your daddy" jousts, so they made up lies and pretended to be people they might have been had their fathers lived with them. The children experienced real problems when changing schools because their whole stories had to be told over again each time they moved, and the leadership issues had to be renegotiated with each new set of kids.

Sherry and I decided we would open a residential care home for boys with the insurance money we received from Kurry's accident. It would be a group home for boys aged 12 to 17. Our goal was to target at-risk boys in our community, give them a home and help them succeed at school. However, we found we had to be licensed by the State of California to realize our dream, and then could receive only those children placed by the state.

Rather than serving only boys in the Modesto area, the boys would come from various counties throughout northern California. We followed the state's guidelines, and Uncle Charlie's Home was approved and licensed by the state of California in June 1985.

I retired from UPS in March 1986 and became the administrator of our realized dream. Ninety-nine percent of the boys we received had one thing in common, they came from fatherless homes. They were insecure and afraid to trust anyone. Out of fear, they became verbally abusive, often using violent aggression as a defense to hide their insecurities.

We wanted to provide a safe place for boys to live, a place that could give more than food and shelter, but also a fatherly type of love. We designed a behavior modification program based on family values to motivate boys toward family leadership instead of gang involvement. I felt we were fulfilling an obligation to pass on the beautiful, ancient art of family love that had been given to us by Jab and Cordie, Ma and Paw, and all who came before us.

Initially, I had thought particularly of three of my nephews when I dreamed of Uncle Charlie's Home. Back when Eston was killed, his fiancé was three months pregnant with Eston's son. Eston died in June, and his son was born in December. She named him Eston, Jr. His mother did her best to raise him without a father, but he got into trouble, sneaking away from home to run the streets. He was a teenager, about 14 or 15 now, and his mother couldn't control him. Eston Jr. was one of the main reasons I wanted to start a group home.

In addition, my older sister, Shirley, and her husband had separated, and she was trying to raise their five kids. I wanted to help raise Tyrone, the youngest boy in her family and his older brother, Michael, in Uncle Charlie's home, along with Eston, Jr. I didn't know all the details it would take to be able to help raise my nephews, but my dream originated with them. I wanted to raise these three, and perhaps other nephews, which is how I'd chosen the name Uncle Charlie's Home.

At any rate, Tyrone and Eston were the only ones who came. The state placed Eston because he'd been in juvenile hall. When I went to get him out, I found out about having to have a license and insurance and the other requirements of the state to run Uncle Charlie's Home. It took a year to get all the necessary details set up. Then, once we'd opened it, we could only take the children the state approved, so I couldn't take my nephews as I'd planned.

Tyrone wanted to come anyway, so I took him into my own home. He didn't move out until he turned 28 years old. Sherry and I put him through school.

Eston Jr. ran away from Uncle Charlie's, too, taking off after only a day. He stayed only for a small while at Uncle Charlie's Home. Then one day he ran away and didn't come back.

However, after a while he met a girl that he loved. I found out because Eston began calling me for advice. Finally, one day Eston called and asked if I would perform a wedding for them. I married them to each other in Manteca, a town just north of Modesto.

Eston and his wife waited to have children until they'd been married for about five years. Then they had three children, whom they're raising in a Christian home. Eston works and is a family man. Somehow, Eston credits this all to Uncle Charlie, who at the beginning, didn't see how I was doing anything good for the boy.

In addition to my nephews, about 150 boys lived in Uncle Charlie's Home over the twelve years it existed. Most of them had been in juvenile hall or were on their way, because they had given up trying to live within cultural boundaries. They used language and violence to combat what they saw as other children picking on them. Often they were moved from one school to another, sometimes several schools in one year.

The beginning of the behavioral modification program at Uncle Charlie's stabilized a boy in one school. In order to do that, I became their security blanket at school. When they had problems I would go down as their advocate, so they'd have someone to turn to. Sherry and I also persuaded the boys to go to church.

We brought teachers, psychologists and other trained personnel into the home, and at one time Uncle Charlie's was a Level 10 home.

However, the dream I had had didn't include professional people. These people could get jobs anywhere they wanted to. My dream had been to hire some of the single mothers trying to raise children on welfare. I wanted to hire and train them so they could have better jobs, learn more about caring for their children and stabilizing their families, then move on and do better things with their lives. I hired some of them. However, when the state evaluated Uncle Charlie's Home, they found this "untrained" staff, and fined the home $25,000. I appealed several times, but finally paid

$10,000 to the state and was forgiven the rest. Working with the children was not the problem that keeping trained staff and fighting the government were.

The children were challenging, but their lives were the reward. At fourteen, a boy named Melvin came to Uncle Charlie's Home. He stayed for about a year and a half.

He came right out of the ghetto in Oakland. His mother and her sisters were on drugs. I took him to visit his family now and then. The state didn't require me to take children more than 25 miles from home, but I took him anyway. As soon as Melvin got out of the car each time, he was free to do whatever he wanted to do. His mother acted totally unconcerned. He would go out the back door, meet his friends and be gone. However, I would tell him when he had to be back, and he would be there. He was one of those kids who only wanted a father. I tried to be that father for him. Melvin would go to school and get in a fight with some other kid. I would go talk to the teacher and apologize to the principal, and Melvin loved being someone's child.

Unfortunately, Melvin had become exceptional at stealing cars. He hot-wired most of them. One day he stole a brand new Toyota Camry that someone leased. The owners had left the keys in the car, so Melvin went by and took the keys in the daytime. The people locked the car again, but it still sat in their driveway.

At night Melvin went back and drove the car away. Down the street from Uncle Charlie's Home stood an empty house, and Melvin parked the car there.

I was leaving Uncle Charlie's to drive home that night about 8:00. I thought it strange to see a car parked in the driveway of a home where no one lived, but gave it no further thought. Later that same night, about 1:00 a.m., the housemother from Uncle Charlie's called and said, "Melvin is gone."

I said, "OK, I'll drive around and see if I can find him." As I drove by the vacant house, I noticed the Camry gone, but

I still didn't give it much thought. Although I knew Melvin didn't like to walk at night much.

A little later, I drove by Franklin School, and there sat the Camry parked in the parking lot. All the lights were out at the school. Strange. I turned around and drove up next to the Camry, got out and looked in the window. There was Melvin lying on the floorboard, hiding.

I motioned for Melvin to get out of the Camry. I said, "Melvin, we've got to take this car back. I'm going to call the cops to keep you from getting into trouble."

I called the police, who said," We haven't had any report of the car being stolen."

Nevertheless, the officers came out and told Melvin and I, "If you take it back and lock it up, assuming the people don't say anything, we won't say anything, either."

I couldn't let Melvin take it back since he wasn't licensed to drive, so I found another driver to take it back. We parked it right in the driveway where it had been stolen, put the keys on the floorboard, locked it up, and never heard anything from the owners about it.

I went home and said, "Melvin, when I was a kid, and I'd do something like this, my father would whip my butt. And that's what I'm going to do to you."

I took him down to the church, marched him into the office, took off his belt and whipped Melvin's butt. This, of course, was illegal. However, that's what did it for Melvin.

Melvin is now 29, and likely to pop in at my house any day, saying, "Hi, Uncle Charlie!" He lives in Sacramento, and manages the tire sales at Costco. I said to him one day, "Melvin, you don't have to call me *Uncle* Charlie."

Melvin replied, "I want to call you Uncle Charlie. You're the only man who ever whipped my butt. I needed it, too."

Another boy, Ron Masterson, a half Cuban, half white boy, stayed the longest at Uncle Charlie's Home. His mother had given him up as a baby, but he came to Uncle Charlie's

Image OF A Black Father

Home from an orphanage when he was twelve years old. He lived there until he turned 19. During that time his mother would visit him about once a year. In one of those years, Ron prayed to ask Jesus to guide his life. Finally, he went through high school graduation and it became time for him to go out into the world.

About two months before Ron graduated I bought him a $5000 Globe Life Insurance policy. It's the kind where a person sends $1 and doesn't have to send anymore for six months. I sent them $1 for insurance on Ron because he was getting ready to try his wings. I also enrolled Ron at ITT, a tech school in Phoenix, Arizona, and we flew down to find him a place to stay. He was all set, and we flew home to Modesto.

While Ron waited to go to Arizona, I rented him a little house in the back of Uncle Charlie's Home as transitional housing, for which Ron never got to pay any rent. One day he went out riding his bike with earphones on. He came up to the railroad crossing at I Street in Modesto, stopping right on the railroad track waiting for the arm to go up. He apparently didn't realize he had stopped on the track itself. At 19 years old, the train hit and killed him. We'd had such hopes for the boy.

I sent Ron's death certificate to Globe Insurance, and the company sent me $5000. I didn't know where Ron's mother lived. Her husband had left her when Ron was born, and she had moved to Colorado. That's the last place I'd known her to reside. I searched and finally found her in El Cajon, California. I told her what had happened and offered to send her a train ticket to come for the funeral. She said, "I'm married now, could you send a ticket for my husband, too."

I saw that they both got to Modesto, and had a room in a local motel. Their meals were paid for, and because she was actually homeless and had no clothes for the funeral, Sherry took her shopping. At any rate, with the cost of getting Ron's mother to the funeral, caring for her while she stayed in Modesto, and the funeral itself, we had only a little over $200 left of the insurance money. We gave that to Ron's mother and sent her home. She still calls now and then.

Uncle Charlie's Home closed in 1997 because of the troubles with the state and more with the county.

LOSING A HERO

Late winter or early spring, depending on the weather, is the time when the farmer breaks ground. He plows the field to prepare it for planting. During this time of year in 1992 Dad went out to clear his backyard, pull weeds, space the ground, and prepare for planting his annual vegetable garden. That same evening after dinner he suffered a stroke. He lost his voice, and the left side of his body fell limp. The ambulance took him to Doctor's Hospital on a Friday. The following day, he seemed fine. He had regained his speech and mobilization of his body.

I asked, "How are you doing?"

Dad said, "I feel fine. In fact, I haven't felt bad through the whole thing. I just have no control of my faculties. I'm not dizzy, I just can't work my muscles. I could have died with no pain, and I certainly have no fear of dieing."

Dad's doctor told him he would be coming home on Saturday if there were no further complications.

Sometime in his sleep on Friday night, he suffered another stroke that rendered him immobile, speechless, and unable to swallow without difficulty. He remained in the hospital for several days with no pain, no fear, but no response. His body was old and tired. It had decided to stop.

The family brought him home. He refused to eat or drink anything. He would accept only chipped ice into his mouth. By now there were six generations in Jab's family. His offspring numbered more than 100 members. He gave them all ample time to visit with him. Pauline, his firstborn, from Ohio, arrived last. It seemed as though he waited for her. She arrived on a Tuesday, and he departed the following day. Seven of his nine kids were with him. Pauline and Charlie were with him in the bedroom while Dot and the others visited with Cordie in the living room. Jab didn't want Cordie to see him die.

    A sweet aroma filled the house that night. There was joy and laughter, light joking and singing. The family felt the love they always felt when they came together. Jab lay motionless on his bed. Pauline sat at his right side; I stood on his left holding his hand and assuring him that I would care for Mom. Jab's debts were paid, and he had nothing obligating him to stay.

    He breathed heavily, and slightly closed his watery eyes like an exhausted child wanting to sleep. I started singing to him. He opened his eyes wide and stared at the ceiling for about 30 seconds. His eyes were now very clear. He looked surprised, but not frightened. Then slowly he closed his eyes and hushed his breathing. The sharecropper died the same way he lived, without complaining.

    The sweet aroma did not leave the room. The silence sounded beautiful. Pauline stroked his hair, and I still held his hand. Neither of us felt sorrow. Not only had he shown them how to live, but he had shown them how to die. Death without pain was his reward for a life well lived. I could almost see his footprints leading up that furrow into Heaven, and I hoped to follow those footprints, to be a sharecropper, too.

CHAPTER THIRTEEN

Memorial to the Sharecropper

The bell tolled solemnly inside the gray brick steeple as I joined others walking toward Greater True Light Baptist Church in the spring sunshine of a San Joaquin Valley morning. The simple, low one-note tones of the bell and the sound of my feet hitting the pavement set me thinking about my father's life. The man I had learned life from, now lay in a casket inside the church. Dad had never been a politician or public servant of any kind. He'd never served in the military or even participated in a high school rally. Never rich or popular by any means, he had labored as a sharecropper, a poor, old sharecropper, whom very few people had the privilege of knowing.

Nevertheless, Dad's funeral today would surely be large. People joined my approach to the church from both sides of the street, down the short sidewalk. Cars filled the parking lot, and more parked in the dirt at the sides of Harris Street for several blocks.

Image OF A Black Father

Walking among the people just ahead of me were the Marino brothers from Dos Palos, standing out like coffee with too much cream in a sea of black.

Dad had farmed his last working days, along with me and most of my brothers and sisters, for the Marino brothers twenty years ago. These men, experienced, educated cotton growers, had taken time out of their lives and lain aside their race and cultural differences to help Jab Crane's family and friends remember him. They'd come 65 miles from Dos Palos to Modesto, California, white folks, coming to a black church because of the love and respect they had for my father. His strong but gentle way of living the long, hard, bitter life he had been given endeared him to everyone. He had left a soft, sweet impact in the Marino brothers' hearts and in the hearts of all he met.

I walked past the pictures of Dad in the foyer. Could this man, who had been such a vital part of my life, really be gone? Inside, the pews had filled to bursting. In the front were my mother, Cordie, and the nine living of my 94 year-old father's thirteen children. They sat with their kids and grandkids.

Before I took my place with my wife, Sherry, and our children among the family members, I walked over to say one last goodbye to Dad. He lay there in his casket looking 75, not 94, and at rest at last. He looked a lot like me. His barely wrinkled, coffee hewed face, his square jaw still looked strong to me, even lying there in the casket. Dad had never stopped, never shuffled his feet. He had been active and spry to the very end of his life.

Pastor Tim Simmons strode straight and tall to the pulpit gathering himself to speak. I felt sympathy for Pastor Simmons in this difficult task. He had loved Jab, too. How he began struck my heart. The pastor said, "St. Claire (Jab) Crane did not have opportunity to attend school as a child – but his children did. He never received a diploma – but his children did. This man never served in the military or went off to war for his country – but four of his seven sons did. This man lived long enough to see the positive fulfillment of life in his children.

"Mr. Crane was 32 when he married his wife, Cordie. He already had a daughter, Pauline, seven, from a previous marriage. Pauline is here with us today. He told me he had a third-grade education and worked at the cotton gin in Dumas, Arkansas in those early days for fifty cents a day, twelve-hour days. Jab and Cordie had 13 children. Some have gone on, but those living are here with us today."

As Pastor Simmons spoke, I looked over at Mom. She didn't ever remember a time in her life when Jab was *not* there. I remembered so many good times between them, and I wasn't even their oldest child.

My mind wandered back to when Jab was about 75. He had planted a pecan tree in his backyard.

I was over at their house one day having coffee with them in the kitchen when they started a discussion about the pecan tree.

"How long will it take for the tree to bear?" Mom asked Dad.

"About seven years," Dad answered.

"Too bad you won't get a chance to eat any," she said, laughing. Dad just smiled.

About ten years later I was over there again when Jab, the muscles in his arms bulging, sweat darkening his shirt down the middle of his back, carried in several boxes filled with nuts. He had climbed up in the tree himself and thrashed them down.

Cordie, amazed, asked, "Did you get all those nuts from that one tree?"

Jab smiled and softly replied, "This is only my half. Your half is still up in the tree."

In later years, Cordie'd call me and say, "Charlie, you've got to come and get this old man out of the pecan tree. He's going to fall and break himself to pieces!"

I'd say, "Mom, he's not going to listen to me."

She'd reply, "Well, come anyway. He's not listening to me!"

When I'd pull up in front of their house, I'd just barely be able to see Dad, up about 40 feet off the ground, perched on a limb.

"The Spiritulaires will sing Jab's favorite song, *Nearer My God to Thee*," Pastor Simmons said, rousing me from my reverie.

The four of us climbed the steps to the stage. I stood straight, in honor of Dad, but I sang softly, around the knot in my throat, and I didn't look at Mom.

Her marriage to Dad had lasted for 62 years, all of Cordie's adult life. Mom and Dad had married in Dumas, Arkansas, like Pastor Simmons had said. It was a one-dog town with only one main street, home to two grocery stores, one of them Chinese, a movie theatre and a filling station. Cordie was only 16 years old, had finished eighth grade and was working in the cotton fields with her parents, Bud and Lucinda Jackson.

I remembered Dumas, even though we moved when I was small. White people in Dumas tolerated "colors" as long as they stayed in their "place," and their place had been clearly marked. On all public facilities throughout the town there were signs stating their use, that said, "white men only," "white women only," or "colored." All drinking fountains were marked "white only." In Arkansas, there was total segregation in the schools, hospitals, police department and even in the church. All social activities or services were withheld from coloreds. Colored people tolerated these living arrangements because they knew of no other way.

Image OF A Black Father

Dad had told me about the days before he was born in Dumas. Jab and Cordie made a promise in the presence of God to love and to cherish each other in sickness and in health, in prosperity and in adversity. They promised to be to each other in all things true and faithful and to cleave unto each other as long as they both should live. Then they started making their own living arrangements together.

And now, today, this must be the saddest day in Cordie's life, I thought. Trying to say goodbye to Jab, she was shaking her head left and right saying, "Lord, Lord, Lord – Lord have mercy," not in denial or disbelief, but wonderment. She must have been wondering, what is life going to be without him?

My mother didn't remember a time in her life when Jab was not there. Charlie knew she was wondering, What will I do when the funeral is over? Who will be there to comfort me when everyone has gone home, after the meal has been eaten, after the grave has been covered, after the last song has been sung, after the preacher finishes his preaching? Who will be there to hold me in the middle of the night? What will happen when I go to that cold, lonely, empty house? It's not a home anymore if Jab is not there. It's not a home.

She never remembered being alone. Through all the rearing of her 12 kids, Jab was there. Through all the heartaches and pain and disappointments, Jab was there. Through all the cold winters in Arkansas, Jab was there. Through the hot long summers, through the cotton picking days, all the times she suffered and was discomfited, Jab was there to console her. Now, Jab was gone. What would she do? Who would she turn to?

Jab had said to her many times, "If anything happens to me, Charlie will take care of you." He had deposited his life savings in Charlie's name for that very purpose.

But I knew my strong-spirited mother was thinking, and she had always told me, "I will never be a burden to my children." Now she was going to have to be a burden to somebody. This bothered her. This bothered her greatly. She continued to shake her head. "Lord, Lord, Lord, oh Lord have mercy."

Pastor Simmons continued his sermon. "We are celebrating the life of a man who has left a good name as an inheritance to his children. A good name is better than riches."

I continued to think, again not hearing the pastor's words, about the good name of a sharecropper. What had Jab's good name done for his life? I thought about all the ways and all the times I had wanted to be just like my father, not in riches, but in a good name – a name that reflected the character, the dignity of a just man, a good name. I thought, *There's a Hebrew idiom that sums it all up. It says a man who shapes and molds the character of someone younger than him, or someone who's under his tutelage, becomes the father of that man, whether he's the biological father or just a father in his experience and teaching. The Hebrews used to take the first-born son at the age of 12 and taught him all he needed to know about his job, about what he would inherit, about the weight he would carry in the family, and how he would be left to support the family when the father had gone on.*

When that young man was fully taught and fully mature around the age of 30, the father turned everything over to his care. Therefore, he was his father's son, an exact replica of what his father really was.

I thought about how *my* father, Jab, had influenced my life, had molded and shaped my character. My physical being was molded and shaped by Jab's seed. We were both 5'8" tall and muscular. Not only my physical self, but my behavior, dignity and character had been shaped by watching my father. I had watched Jab as long as I could remember.

Charlie Crane
313 Melbourne Dr.
Modesto, CA 95357

LaVergne, TN USA
01 February 2010
171729LV00007B/144/A